1   Hint Fuerteventura in a different way

By Andrea Müller

Andrea Müller, Calle Las Cuevas, 91 - A2
E- 35542 Punta Mujeres, province of Las Palmas, Lanzarote
Web: www.fuerteventura-mal-anders.de
mailto:ebook@fuerteventura-mal-anders.de
© 2020 Andrea Müller,
Cover design: Andrea Müller
Number of pages Print variant: 84 pages
Number of images: 18 images/cards

2   Imprint (German)

Bibliographic Information of the German National Library

The German National Library lists this publication in the German National Bibliography; detailed bibliographic data are available on the Internet at http://dnb.d-nb.de

© 2020 Andrea Müller

Production and publishing
BoD - Books on Deman, Norderstedt

ISBN: 9783750460263

3   Fuerteventura - An overview

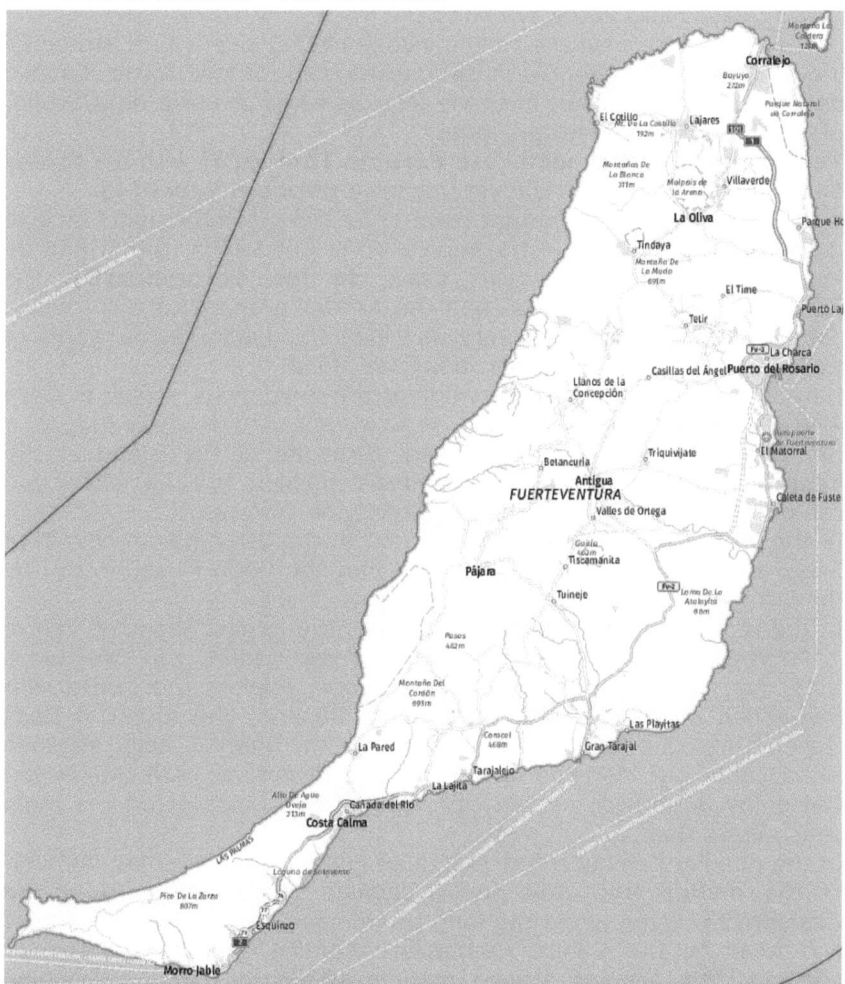

Fuerteventura... different! leads you beside endless long, dreamlike snow-white Caribbean beaches to the worth seeing attractions of the multifaceted volcanic island. In the north, from the largest and liveliest town of **Corralejo[1]** with its beautiful dunes, explore the small nature reserve **Isla Los Lobos[2]**, where the former lighthouse keeper runs a small restaurant, and enjoy the beautiful beaches of the Playas Grandes, which are particularly suitable for water sports in the sections Flag Beach, Playa Bajo Negro, Playa Moro and Playa Poris.

In the northwest, visit the fishing village of El Cotillo, which protected the coast from intruders with its centuries-old fortified tower, Castillo de Testón, and look out over the long beaches of Playa del Castillo, where kite and body-surfers meet.

Make a detour to the lighthouse **Faro de Tostón[3]** with the fishing museum and don't miss the yet unknown **popcorn beach[4].**

Visit the historically important town of La Oliva, whose sights include the parish church of Nuestra Señora de la Candelaria, the Ermita de Puerto Rico, the impressive **Casa de los Coroneles[5]**, the dilapidated Casa del Inglés, and the former granary La Cilla, which dates back to the 17th century. Art lovers can admire the works of well over 80 artists in the spacious Casa Mané.

Marvel at the unique rock carvings of the indigenous people in Casa Alta de Tindaya.

Immerse yourself in the traditional rural life of the island at the **Ecomuseo de La Alcogida[6]** open-air museum in Tefía, where you can purchase genuine handicrafts directly on the spot.

In the little visited village of Tetír, next to the listed parish church of Santo Domingo de Guzman, you will find the Gofio Museum, run by the last active gofio miller in the world.

In the island's capital Puerto del Rosario, the largest shopping centre in Fuerteventura, Las Rotondas, awaits you, where you can buy a wide range of products in specialist shops. Explore the centre with the parish church Nuestra Señora del Rosario, the museum Casa Museo Unamuno, buy local products in the market halls Mercado Municipal or the Mercado Agrario de Fuerteventura. Afterwards you can enjoy a sunbath on the city beach Playa Chica or on the main beach Playa Blanca.

In the popular holiday resort Caleta de Fustes you can enjoy the view of the marina from the gently sloping sandy beach **Playa de Castillo[7].** Stroll along the long promenade past historic lime kilns and head to the Centro Comercial Atlantico shopping centre. In addition, the popular African market allows for further shopping opportunities.

Explore the historic **Salinas del Carmen[8]** with the Museo de La Sal, where salt was actively extracted until 1980.

In the centre of Fuerteventura you will meet even more island history: During a guided tour through La Ampuyenta you will see the small but impressive Ermita de San Pedro de Alcántara and learn all the details in the house Casa Museo Dr. Mena, as well as in the hermitage of Fray Andresito.

In sleepy Antigua, head to the Molino de Antigua windmill and its interesting cheese museum **Museo de Queso Majorero[9]**.

Don't miss a stop in Tuineje to see the altarpieces of the important battle of Tamasite in the church of San Miguel Arcángel.

In Pájara, visit the impressive parish church of Nuestra Señora de la Regla, in front of which stands a Noria, a restored water wheel driven by a donkey.

Drive to the rugged coast of Ajuy with the deep black beach of the dead, the **Playa de Los Muertos[10]** and explore along the sea cliffs the lime kilns, as well as the deep caves Cuevas, which served as a pirates' hideout.

In the former capital of the island **Betancuria[11]**, which belongs to the most beautiful villages of Spain since this year, you should visit the church Nuestra Señora de la Concepción with the attached museum for sacral art and the monastery ruins of the Convento de San Buenaventura with the Ermita San Diego, besides a city tour.

From the 645-metre-high Mirador de Morro Velosa lookout point, you can see the desert-like landscape of the island. You must make selfies at the **Mirador de Guise y Ayose[12]** with its 4.50 m high statues of the former island kings.

You can see how old windmills work on the island in the small museum Centro de Interpretación de Molinos in Tiscamanita.

You can even buy stuffed gofio biscuits on a trip to the Quesos de Belido cheese dairy.

Cross the impassable Malpais of the natives, which is interspersed with rubble and lava stones, and simply turn back time in the stone-built settlement of **La Atalayita[13]**.

If you come across the large holiday resort Las Playitas with a dark, fine sandy beach on the east coast, you must definitely visit the unique lighthouse **Faro Punta de la Entallada[14]**.

In Gran Tarajal you will meet locals who live here and work in the restaurant and hotel industry on the fine sandy dark beach.

You will find an almost German enclave in Tarajalejo with a hotel of the Spanish R2 group and apartments, which runs along the long promenade with a dark pebble beach. Worth mentioning are the new 5 sculptures of the Mareseum.

In La Lajita you should definitely spend a nice day in the huge **Oasis Wildlife Park[15]**, where children will also get their money's worth with the impressive shows.

Let yourself be impressed by the unique contrast of a barren mountainous landscape and a miniature Sahara: Experience a rough coast with beautiful bays in La Pared, at the narrowest point of the island, the Istmo de la Pared, look northwards at the big rock gate, or face the waves of the Atlantic Ocean at the Playa de Viejo Rey. Visit the award-winning cheese dairy La Pastora, which offers sheep and goat cheese and liqueur made from goat's milk.

Feel at home on the Costa Calma, which is preferred by Germans, with a beautiful beach location and guaranteed sunshine. Shop in the shopping malls, stroll through the Africa market or enjoy tapas and typical German cuisine with a freshly tapped Pils.

An absolute must is the more than 20 km long beach section that starts after Costa Calma, leads over Jandía Playa and ends in the former fishing village Morro Jable. Take a break on the snow-white beach with the crystal-clear turquoise sea and simply let your soul dangle.

From Playa de Sotavento to the Risco del Paso, thanks to the René Egli Wind- and Kite Surf Center, beginners and professionals alike will get their money's worth.

Swim in the south of Fuerteventura in the beautiful bays of Playa de Butihondo and Playa de Esquinzo and continue endlessly relaxing beach walks to the south of the island to Morro Jable.

Relax at the Playas de Jandía, go shopping at the long shopping promenade in Jandía and enjoy the most beautiful beach section Playa del Matorral, which is especially suitable for children.

Set off from the harbour town of Morro Jable to the southern tip of Fuerteventura. Reach the sleepy village of Puerto de la Cruz with the lighthouse Faro de Jandíavia jerky volcanic roads. Take the serpentines to Cofete to the endless **Playa de Barlovento [16]** with an incredible surf and visit the historic Villa Winter, where the rumour mill is bubbling.

Space for personal notes...✎...

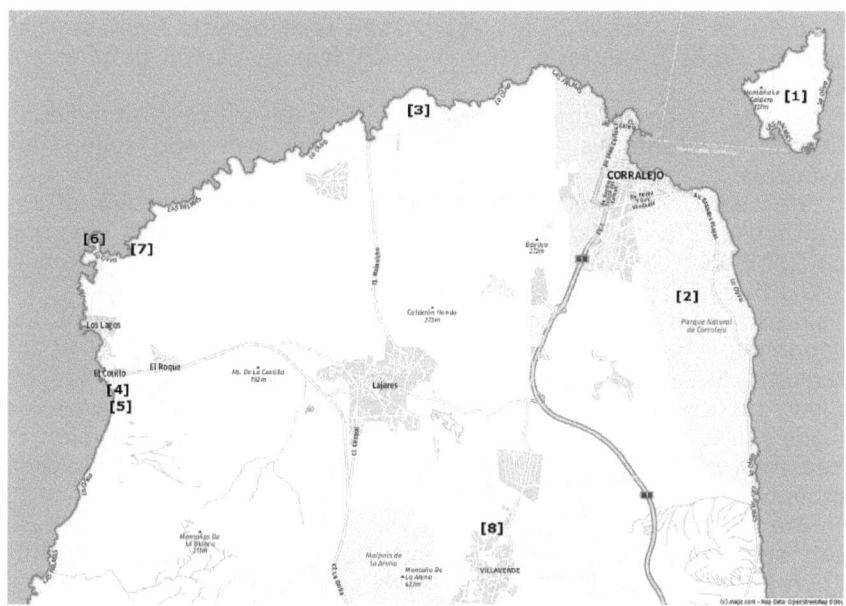

4 La Isla de Los Lobos

The island **Isla de Los Lobos[1], which is** only 6 square kilometres in size, is located between the neighbouring island of Lanzarote and Fuerteventura in the strait of La Bocaina. It was formed by a violent volcanic eruption in northern Fuerteventura about 6,000-8,000 years ago.

Thanks to successful protests, neither building sins nor tourist development measures took place on Los Lobos. In 1982 the island was declared a Parque Natural and in 1987 it was integrated into the Dune National Park of Corralejo.

The name derives from the monk seals Lobos marineros, which romped in the 15th century before and on the island. Fearing dwindling fish stocks, the hunt for the seals was opened, which were then wiped out within a century.

In the year 1863, a lighthouse was built that until today guides the ships between Lanzarote, Fuerteventura and Los Lobos.

After the lighthouse was automated after more than a hundred years in 1968, the island government allowed the lighthouse keeper, who would otherwise have been without employment, to open a fish restaurant in the harbour to earn a living.

In the port of Corralejo, a glass bottom boat departs from the pier several times a day and after only 15 minutes it will dock at Los Lobos.

From the concrete landing stage a path leads to the visitor centre Centro de Visitantes, where information boards and toilets are available.

If you start your hike across the island in the direction of the lighthouse Faro de Martiño, after 10 minutes you will reach the small port of El Puertito with the restaurant of the former lighthouse keeper and a bathing opportunity in the crystal-clear lagoon.

This path continues along ruins of houses to the small lagoons Las Lagunitas. They are characterized by plants that can grow in the region of El Saladar, as in Jandía, in spite of sea water.

Along the seething black coast the following sand track passes and leads you to the lighthouse, which unfortunately is not accessible.

You follow the signs and can then climb the 127 m high volcanic mountain Montaña Caldera in 30-60 minutes.

In the Las Salinas del Carmen salt works, which are signposted, you can see a salt plant that has been restored but never went into operation. On your island tour you will find one of the most beautiful bays of Los Lobos, the Playa de La Calera. Here you can relax and enjoy the sun to the full.

◉daily, upon reservation on the Internet, ①Since the beginning of 2019, there are only limited places to visit Los Lobos. At www.visitaislasdelobos.com you have to register at short notice to be allowed to visit the island.

5   Corralejo

In the 1950s, the still small fishing nest Corralejo with some tiny buildings and only 200 inhabitants developed from the year 1968 to a lively holiday resort in the north of the island.

When the unique, breathtaking **dune landscape [2]**, which is located south of the city, was placed under strict nature protection in 1982, there were already 2 hotel bunkers: the RIU Tres Islas and the RIU Oliva Beach.

The FV-1 road leads through the 20 square kilometre area to the island capital Puerto del Rosario.

At the coast, on more than 7 km of snow-white dream bathing bays were created, which are crossed by black lava tongues. They were created by drifting sand that blew over from the Famara area of the neighbouring island Lanzarote.

In the following years, permits were only issued for the construction of further hotels outside the dunes and south of Corralejo. Meanwhile, the city has more than 20,000 guest beds and, along with Caleta de Fueste in the centre of the island and Jandía in the south, is one of the most visited holiday destinations on the island.

In the ferry harbour Puerto de Corralejo, boats start in order to transfer to the offshore island Los Lobos or to the neighbour island Lanzarote. Alternatively, there is the possibility to take the big ferries from Fred Olsen or Armas to Lanzarote, so that a car can be taken along.

On a clear day you can enjoy a beautiful view of Lanzarote and Los Lobos from the promenade Punta de Corralejo, which runs along the left side of the harbour. To the right of the harbour, the promenade Avenida Maritima begins, which passes countless restaurants and cafés as well as small beach bays.

In the centre of Corralejo the long Avenida Nuestra Señora del Carmen invites you to go shopping. At the end of the village - towards the main beaches of Playas Grandes - you will find Villa Tabaiba Galeria de Arte. It is privately owned and only opened irregularly. Nevertheless, it is worth taking a look over the wall of the estate to admire the works of art. ⌂ Avenida Grandes Playas, 125-Corralejo

On the main beaches of Playas Grandes, which are signposted and located in front of the RIU hotels, the beautiful, snow-white dunes and sandy beaches present themselves in their full glory.

The beach at the RIU hotels can also be reached by public bus or taxi, whereas for the following bays, Playa Bajo Negro, Playa del Moro and Playa del Porís, which are particularly recommended for kite and body surfers, a rental car is recommended.

➊The place name Corralejo is derived from the Spanish word "corral" and describes a round area surrounded by a stone wall where goats were herded or kept. The word "lejos=far away." So Corralejo means the far away pen.

Mercado Baku

The market is located at the Baku water park. The large product selection contains mainly imitations.✪ Tue + Fri 10-14, ⌂ Avenida Nuestra Señora del Carmen, 41-35660 Corralejo

Mercado El Campanario

The large market is located in the Centro Comercial shopping centre El Campanario. Local arts and crafts are offered.✪ Thu + Sun 10-14,

⌂Calle Hibisco,1- 35660 Corralejo, ⓘDuring the market the shops of the center are open.

6 Aqua- Water Park

The 25,000 square metre water park offers 13 water slides, a wave pool, Jacuzzis, children's areas and a restaurant. Sunbeds and parasols are free of charge.ⓘ Opening hours and entrance fees at: www.acuawaterpark.com, ⌂**Avenida** Nuestra Señora del Carmen, 41- 35660 Corralejo

7 Playa de Majanicho and popcorn beach

There are 2 possibilities to reach the beaches. To get to the picturesque **Playa de Majanicho[3]** you have to drive from Lajares in northern direction. ⌂ FV- 109> Roundabout> Calle la Cancela. With a little luck you will see local fishermen preparing their fish for lunch by the sea. Now follow the lower sand track > Calle Majanicho, which is not as jerky as the upper one. After about 10 minutes by car you will find a beach hut that has been boarded up. Directly in front of it is the Popcorn Beach, which lives up to its name. The popcorn is a calcareous algae found in the waters between Lanzarote and Fuerteventura. They are formed at a depth of twenty metres below sea level and grow only about one millimetre per year. When they have died, they are washed to the coasts by the tides, where erosion gradually turns them into sand.
From Corralejo: Coming from the port, on the road to the main bus station Estacion de Autobuses- Avenida Juan Carlos I, you will find the Hotel Bristol Sunset Beach. On the right-hand side there is a signpost with the inscriptions: Estacion de Autobuses, Playas Grandes and Majanicho→. Here you turn directly right into the inconspicuous path where cars are parked at the beginning. Now follow the sand track towards the coast.

8 Lajares

The small village has the charm of a hippie eldorado and is a popular stopover for surfers on their way to the coast to El Cotillo. In the centre of the village there is a small hippie market with handmade souvenirs every Saturday from 10.00-14.00 hours.
Lajares became famous for its Escuela de Artesania Canaria, which has a long tradition of craftsmanship. At the end of the 19th to the beginning of the 20th century, embroidery introduced by Portuguese immigrants was in full bloom. Returnees from America and Portugal

employed the women of the village as cheap labourers who were underpaid due to greed for profit.

The founder of the school, Mrs. Natividad Hernandez Lopez, made sure that the workers were paid fairly and in 1957 she founded the embroidery school to train more women. In the meantime, it has become attached to one of the largest handicraft shops on the island, where handicrafts, aloe vera products, clothing and food are sold. ⌂FV-109, Calle Coronel Glez del Yerro, 14- 35650 La Oliva,⟟ Right next to the pharmacy- Farmacia there is a lottery point which also serves as a souvenir shop.

In the past, in addition to goat farming, cereal farming played an important role in Fuerteventura. In the district of Casas de Arriba there are 2 Canarian gofio windmills, in which the roasted grain was processed into flour. In the large cobbled square is the 18th century church Ermita San Antonio de Padua. ⌂ Calle Central,27- 35650 La Oliva

9   El Cotillo

The village is located at the end of FV-10 on the northwest coast of the island. The former fishing village has been extended by numerous new buildings and apartments. At the entrance to the village, on the sea side, you will find the restored windmill Molino El Roque, which is worth a photo.

In the town of El Tostón, which is signposted, you will see restored lime kilns above the new port, which look like small fortresses. They remind us of the once important economic role of the town.

For a long time, lime production was the most important source of income in Fuerteventura and was mainly sold in Gran Canaria.

The most important historical sight is the signposted **Castillo del Tostón[4]**. The history of the defence tower begins with the conquest of the island by the Spanish crown. The bastion was built in the 17th century on the ruins of the old Castillo Rico Roque with stones from a nearby cave. The aim was to protect the coast and the harbour from the frequent attacks of the North African pirates, English and French. The tower has a diameter of 15 m and tapers upwards. In the basement was the powder magazine. On the roof 3 iron cannons and a water cistern were placed, which enabled the 12 soldiers to be self-sufficient for a longer period of time.☉ Mon-Fri 9-16, Sat + Sun 9-15 o'clock,⚫2,00 €, children under 12 years free, payment only by credit card. By the way: there is an identical fortified tower in Caleta de Fueste at the Barceló hotel complex, but it is not accessible. Not far from the Castillo del Tostón there is a whale skeleton. Behind it, the more than 1 km long beaches of **Playa del Castillo**begin **[5]**. They are one of the biggest attractions of the town and a popular meeting point for body and kite surfers.

At the northern edge of the village is the small church Ermita de Nuestra Señora del Buen Viaje. The simple building was built in 1834 and has a tiny bell frame on the left side. ⌂ Calle Isla los Lobos,52- 35650 El Cotillo

From El Cotillo the northern coastal road leads to the fishing museum Museo de la Pesca Tradicional with the red and white striped lighthouse **Faro El Tostón[6]**. On this way, there is the playa Los Lagos de Cotillo, that is located at the end of the village. After that, the popular beach Playa de La Concha follows. Follow the road until you reach the Caleta del Rio. In 1897, construction work began on the original lighthouse with an outbuilding for the lighthouse keeper, which has since been converted into a fishing museum. The lighthouse was used to mark the sea area from the Ballena headland and marks the Bocaina strait between Fuerteventura and Lanzarote.

In the middle of the 20th century, because of the low height and the dilapidation of the old tower, it was decided to build a new higher lighthouse, which was inaugurated in 1955.

The new red and white striped tower is operated automatically and has a height of 30 m. Its range is 14 nautical miles, which corresponds to about 26 km. The lighthouse keeper of the La Entallada lighthouse, located to the south near Las Playitas, carries out the work necessary for maintenance and operation.

The museum is dedicated to the fishing industry and its importance for Fuerteventura with Spanish-English pictures and inscriptions. A German, 30-page information booklet is available at the entrance.

✪Tue-Sat 10-17, ❶Please note that toilets are available but cannot be used. Also the old lighthouse is no longer accessible. Tip: If you would like to stretch your legs after a long journey, a 30-minute signposted walk around the lighthouse is a good idea. Further dreamlike bathing bays, like the **Playas de Los Charcos[7]**, are located not far from the lighthouse, in northern direction.

10 Villaverde

In the centre of the village is the small 18th century church Ermita de San Vicente Ferrer de Villaverde. The main portal is at the back. ⌂Calle Francisco Bordon Mendez, 59- 35640 La Oliva

The place would be more worth visiting if the main attraction, the cave **Cueva del Llano[8],** was still open. It was formed about 1 million years ago when a lava flow cooled from the outside and a lava flow leaked from the inside. With a length of 648 m and a diameter of 7 to 10 m it is the largest cave on the island. It has been closed since 2017, as the endangered spider species "Maiorerus randoi", which is native to Fuerteventura and threatened with extinction, lives here in the rear part, which is inaccessible to humans.

The endemic spider species was first discovered in 1991. It is a remarkable example of the adaptation of living beings to absolute darkness. It is estimated that 20 specimens of the spider, which is only 2.2 mm in size, still exist. The darkness led to the loss of all pigmentation and regression of the eyes, so that the spiders are blind. Their long legs and antennas are thin and serve exclusively for orientation. Genetic studies have shown that this spider species originally came from Africa, probably arrived in Fuerteventura on flotsam and developed into an independent species. In the course of time all other species may have become extinct due to increasing drought on the island. Due to the constant temperatures and high humidity in the Cuevas de Llanos, these few specimens survived.
⌂FV-101, direction Villaverde, signposted from the main road

Space for personal notes...✐...

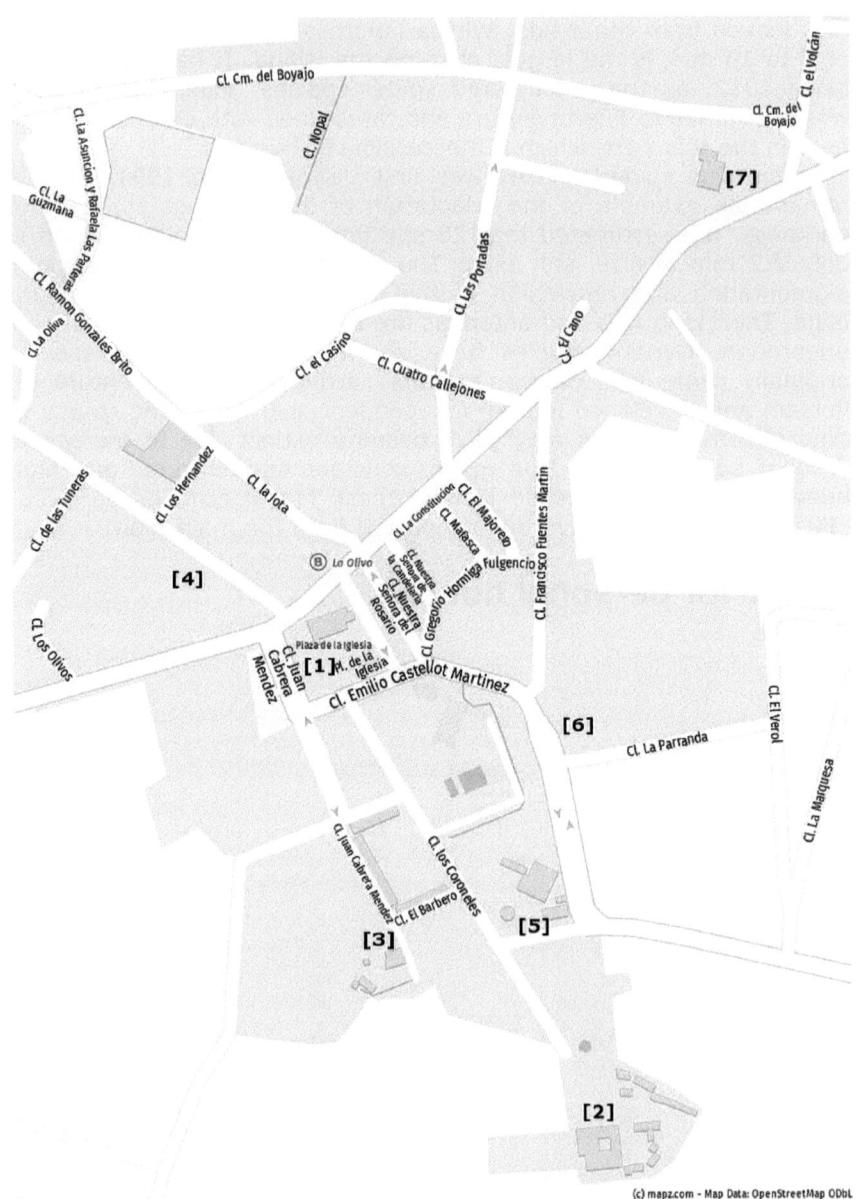

11 La Oliva

At that time, the village of La Oliva was surrounded by olive groves, which led to its name. After the conquest of the Canary Islands, the military regiment controlled the island from here. In the centre is the church **Iglesia Nuestra Señora de La Candeleria[1]**.

It is one of the largest churches in Fuerteventura and has been modified several times over the centuries.

In the 17th century, the church was built when the wealthy bourgeoisie settled in the north of the island. The plain white main façade has three naves with gable roofs. The adjoining bell tower, made of dark lava stone blocks, has a square ground plan and also took on the function of a watchtower to warn the inhabitants of possible pirate attacks. Inside, 5 oil paintings decorate the main altar. They are attributed to the painter Juan de Miranda, who was considered the most important painter of the Canary Islands in the 18th century. The paintings depict San Juan Bautista- Saint John the Baptist, San José con el niño- Saint Joseph with the Child, El Calvario- the Way of the Cross, San Juan Evangelista- Saint John the Evangelist and the Virgen de La Dolorosa- the Virgin of Sorrows.

Records from the early 17th century describe that due to lack of rain, the statue of the Virgin of Candelaria was brought to La Oliva several times in processions to ask for the long-awaited rain.

The church of La Oliva experienced its heyday at the end of the 17th to the middle of the 19th century, when the nobility and the wealthy bourgeoisie entered into the sacred state of marriage. The nobles of the north also found their final resting place here. The last coronel of the island, colonel Cristóbal Manrique de Lara at the age of 32 years married his 16-year-old niece Maria de Las Nieves on 30.03.1834.◐Daily 09-20 o'clock,① The church lighting is attached on the right at the entrance and can be switched on for a fee, ⌂Plaza de La Iglesia, 2- 35640 La Oliva

The historic house **Casa de Los Coroneles[2]** is situated in front of the 326 m high volcanic mountain Montaña Oliva. The estate dates from the 2nd half of the 17th century and is the largest estate in the Canary Islands. This was the residence of the military regime led by the first colonel Ginés de Cabrera Bethencourt, who settled in La Oliva with his family in 1708. He appropriated vast lands and gained increasing political influence, so that he eventually owned a third of the island.

The huge house was said to have a window for each day, 365, but in reality there are only 117. Since the farmers could neither read, write nor calculate, they tried to express the size and fascination of the building in this way.

Until 1994 the manor house was owned by the community of heirs of the descendants. It was bought by the island government and extensively restored from 2001 to 2006.☺ Tue-Sat 10am-6pm, Mon + Sun + Sun + Sun closed,🍴 3,00 €, ⌂sign posted- Calle Los Coroneles, 28- 35640 La Oliva

The **Ermita de Puerto Rico[3]** is absolutely inconspicuous, but steeped in history. It was the first chapel in the community where the Christian inhabitants prayed. Worth seeing are the elaborate stonemasonry work on the lateral portal and the window surrounds.

Not far from the Iglesia Nuestra Señora de La Candeleria is the restored grain museum **Casa de La Cilla[4]**. It dates back to the beginning of the 19th century and is housed in the municipality's former granary, in order to highlight the special importance of ancient Canarian cereal products. At that time, the church's harvests were stored in the storehouses, which came from the church's own property and from cent taxes. There were other granaries in the municipalities of Betancuria, Tiscamanita, Tetir and Tindaya.

Until the middle of the penultimate century, the islanders were engaged in the cultivation of cereals, which was Fuerteventura's main economic activity. The fertile valleys and plains of the island were divided into lands and settled, thus ensuring food and trade. Besides wheat, barley, rye, legumes and maize, fruit trees were also cultivated. In rainy years, the harvest was very successful and considerable quantities were sold. However, in years with little rain and no significant crop yields, the island was literally transformed into a poorhouse. As a result, the farmers developed special techniques to make the best possible use of the precious water when it rains. Depending on the work involved, wage labourers were also employed, who were paid with money or a share of grain. The food for the workers, which was paid for by the farmers, consisted of mojo sauces, bread, gofio, figs and salted fish. As drinks there was water and wine. ① With the help of display boards, photographs and antique landscape equipment, you will get a small insight into the primitive work processes of that time. As the exhibition is exclusively labelled in Spanish, you will receive a booklet with the German translations at the box office,☺ Tue-Sat 10- 17.30, 🍴1,50€ ⌂ Calle La Orilla, 5 - 35640 La Oliva

An absolute MUST for lovers of modern art is the **Centro de Arte Canario Casa Mané[5]**. The building has a traditional, simple floor plan. Until the middle of the 19th century it was the residence of Blas Curbelo Guerra, the personal physician of Coronel Cristóbal Manrique de Lara and his family. The center was founded in 1991 through the private initiative of the art dealer Manuel Delgado Camino, who was called Mané. In the meantime, the works of well over 80 artists are exhibited.⓵ As an art lover, you should plan several hours for the worth seeing and extensive exhibition.◷Mon-Fri 10-17, Sat 10-14h,♨ 5,00 €, ⌂Calle Salvador Manrique de Lara- 35640 La Oliva

The traditional market **Mercado de las Tradiciones[6]** is a highlight for authentic souvenirs from Fuerteventura. The building was owned by the colonels of La Oliva. In 1840, Sebastiana Cabrera gave the estate to her son Pedro Manrique de Lara, who led an independent life here. In addition to costume jewellery, wood, silver and leather work, mojos, jams, regional fruit and vegetables are offered.◷ Tue+Fr 10-14, ⌂Calle Francisco Fuentes Martín, 15-35640 La Oliva

The dilapidated manor house **Casa del Inglés[7]** is one of the last testimonies of the wealthy upper class of the village. The two-storey property dates from the 18th century and had an inner courtyard with an underground water reservoir, which was an absolute luxury in times of water shortage.

Currently, the rich builder Julian Leal Sicilia operated a thriving agricultural cultivation and numerous trade activities between the Canary Islands and America. Financial losses led to the sale of his property, which was purchased by the English naturalist Mr. David Parkinson.

When he returned to his home after years, he sold the house, which was then used for different purposes. During the Spanish Civil War - Guerra Civil - it was occupied by the army and served as a sick bay for the local armed forces.

As after years the population only remembered that an Englishman lived in the house, the ruin is called Casa del Inglés- the house of the Englishman. ⌂ FV- 101, km 2, La Oliva to Villaverde

⓵Ruta de Los Coroneles: During a guided tour of the city you can visit the Casa de La Cilla, the Iglesia de La Candelaria, the Casa de Los Coronelles, the Centro de Arte- Casa Mané and the Mercado de Las Tradiciones.

◷ . Tue+Fri 10-14,♨8,00 €, ⌂ Meeting point: Plaza de La Iglesia, at the building on the right side of the church. The tours are conducted in English and Spanish. On Fridays the guides wear traditional costumes.

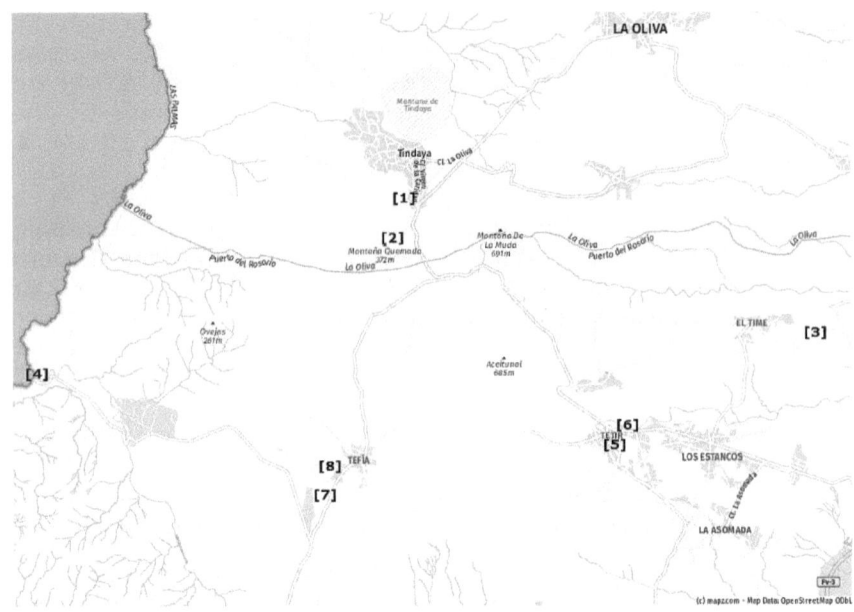

12 Tindaya

The 400 m high Montaña de Tindaya is the holy mountain of the natives of Fuerteventura, where they had a cult and burial place. More than 200 rock carvings in the form of foot outlines were discovered here. Due to repeated vandalism and careless hikers, many of the carvings were irreparably destroyed, so that the island government has imposed an absolute ban on climbing the Tindaya.

Since the mining of the volcanic rock for house building was only stopped after long protests by conservationists, the quarry's excavation sites can still be clearly seen on the slope of the Tindaya. At the edge of the entrance to the village, after the Centro Cultural, there is a small chapel with an open belfry made of black stone. At the end of the village you will find the cheese dairy Quesos de Tindaya, where goat cheese is offered from Monday to Saturday from 08.30 to 14.00 hours.

Not far from FV-10 is the restored building **Casa Alta de Tindaya[1]** with exhibition rooms.

It is dedicated to the artist and sculptor Eduardo Chillida, who has since died. He planned to drill two long vertical light shafts into the volcanic mountain Tindaya and to connect them with an already existing tunnel, which should serve as access. The shafts should be located on the front and back side of the mountain to present the different light play of sun and moon to the visitor. Although the project was intended to be on the opposite side of the rock carvings, it was not implemented.

In the first exhibition room, light plays are simulated in shaft models. In the second room, a large wooden model of the volcanic mountain illustrates the artist's intention; in addition, several dismantled stone blocks with rock carvings are shown. The exhibition is completed by film screenings.◉ Tue-Sun 10-14,🕯 free, ⌂FV-10, Tindaya, 15- 35649 Tindaya

Next to the Casa Alta de Tindaya a gravel road leads to the monument **Monumento Unamuno[2]**. On the occasion of the 100th anniversary, the island government erected a monument in honour of the important Spanish poet and writer Miguel Unamuno in the volcanic mountain of Montañas Quemada, located not far from Tindaya. The mountain was chosen because Unamuno described in one of his letters to a trusted friend that this region was one of the places where he would like to be buried after his death.

13   Casas de Felipito

The **Casas de Felipito[3]** is located in the Llano del Triguero, the plain of the cereal. It was named after Felipe Ruíz Gonzáles, who was called Felipito el feo- the little ugly Philip. He was a farmer and lived here with his parents at the beginning of the 20th century.

To the right of the entrance there is a two-storey building representing a typical country house of modest farmers. After restoration, the complex was opened as a museum in 2002 and is used by islanders as an amusement park with covered, wind-protected seating, barbecue areas, children's playground and bowling alleys.

Remarkable were the enormous efforts that the farmer made at that time to cultivate the land and make it fertile. He used limestone to build walls as wind protection and up to 3 m high enclosures for animals. He also designed drainage systems to channel rainwater onto his property. The ugly Phillipp had the dubious honour of being the first majorero to die in the hospital Viejo- the old hospital, now the University of Fuerteventura.

◉Tue-Sun 8-20,🕯 free, ⌂ Camino Guisguey Puerto de Rosario- 35612 Puerto del Rosario. FV-10 Puerto del Rosario- direction Tetír. At the height of La Asomada take the FV- 219 direction El Time. Follow the signs - about 15 minutes driving time on a gravel road.

14 Puertito de los Molinos

The FV- 221 leads past a wide gorge, which in rainy seasons leads the water from the volcanic mountains into the sea to **Puertito de los Molinos[4].** After heavy rainfall the area is beautifully green, but in summer the play of colours fades.

Once in the harbour, you cross a bridge under which ducks have nested and come across small fishermen's houses.

The most beautiful view over the bay can be enjoyed by walking up the path on the left side of the parking lot. On the rugged rock you can still see the remains of the windmills that gave the village its name.

The dark stone and pebble beach Playa los Molinos is not suitable as a bathing beach due to undercurrents and waves.

15 Tetír

The small village is located on the FV-10 at the height of Puerto del Rosario. Even from a distance you can see the seven-storey bell tower of the parish church of **Santo Domingo de Guzmán[5]**. The church dates back to the 18th century and was declared a protected monument after renovation work that brought to light old murals.

Directly at the main street is the Gofio- **Museum Museo de Gofio[6]**. The owner Francisco Cabrera Oramas is the last active gofio miller. Gofio is a flour made from roasted corn and was the staple food in the Canary Islands. Here history meets production. During a short tour you will learn more about the production. ① All information in the museum is in Spanish, the miller also speaks only Spanish. Only after the arrival of groups the grinding is demonstrated. By calling 639752848, you can ask your hotel reception when the miller will grind gofio. Even without visiting the museum, you can buy freshly ground gofio at the cash desk.◐Mon + Sun 10-15, Tue-Sat 9.30-17 hrs,◗with costs, ⌂ FV-10- Tetír- House number 16- 35613 Puerto del Rosario.

16 Tefía

The open-air museum **Ecomuseo La Alcogida[7]** is the highlight of the village where you can experience the traditional country life. It was inhabited until the end of the 1970s and was then restored by the island government in accordance with the original. The complex consists of seven estates. You will see mansions of wealthy families and simple buildings of modest farmers. Each estate bears the name of the former owners. In the home of Señora Hermina and Señor Donato you will have an insight into the primitive living conditions of the farmers. These houses have a U- or L-shaped ground plan. The inner courtyard faces south. Thick walls of limestone served as wind protection.

Wealthy families had several outbuildings, which were accessed by a wooden or stone staircase. Covered balconies and surrounding wooden galleries reflect the wealth.

In the houses of the Herrera and Cabra families and the miller, the traditional craftsmanship of the island lives on.① Basket weavers, potters, weavers, embroiderers and stonemasons work here every day. The individual handicrafts can be purchased directly from the artist on site. In the building with the signposted "Recepcion" you will receive the entrance tickets and a plan of the tour.◐ Tue- Sa 10-18,⬤ 5.00€, △ FV- 207- Tefía

Also worth seeing is the picturesque windmill of the type **Molina[8]**, which is located directly at the FV-207. Directly opposite, the road leads into the eastern part of the village to the Ermita de San Agustín, which is surrounded by a high wall. The church dates from the early 18th century and has been listed as a historical monument. To the left is the Arena Lucha Canaria, where Canarian wrestling matches are held. △ Calle Lugar Tefia, 32- 35611 Puerto del Rosario

17 Puerto del Rosario

Puerto del Rosario is the capital of the island. Fuerteventura has a total of 115,000 inhabitants, 36,000 of whom live in the capital.

Even before the conquest of the island, the city was recorded on a Venetian nautical chart in 1426. The port served primarily as a loading point for goats, which were loaded as live food on overseas voyages. For this reason, the current Puerto del Rosario wasthen called Puerto de las Cabras - goat port. At the beginning of the 19th century, the English already used the port as a base to control trade with Gran Canaria and the European mainland. Almost immediately, Puerto de las Cabras separated from its mother parish in Tetír and chose the Rosary Madonna Virgen del Rosario as the patron saint for the newly built parish church. Already at that time there was a brisk trade in soda, lime, goats and the red dye from the cochineal louse breeding, so that the port was named the capital of the island. Only in the year 1956 the city was allowed to rename itself after the name of its patron saint in Puerto del Rosario.

Discover the most beautiful sides of the capital with a tour. Best and free parking is available at the port along the Avenida de los Reyes de España.

18   General map Puerto del Rosario Fuerteventura

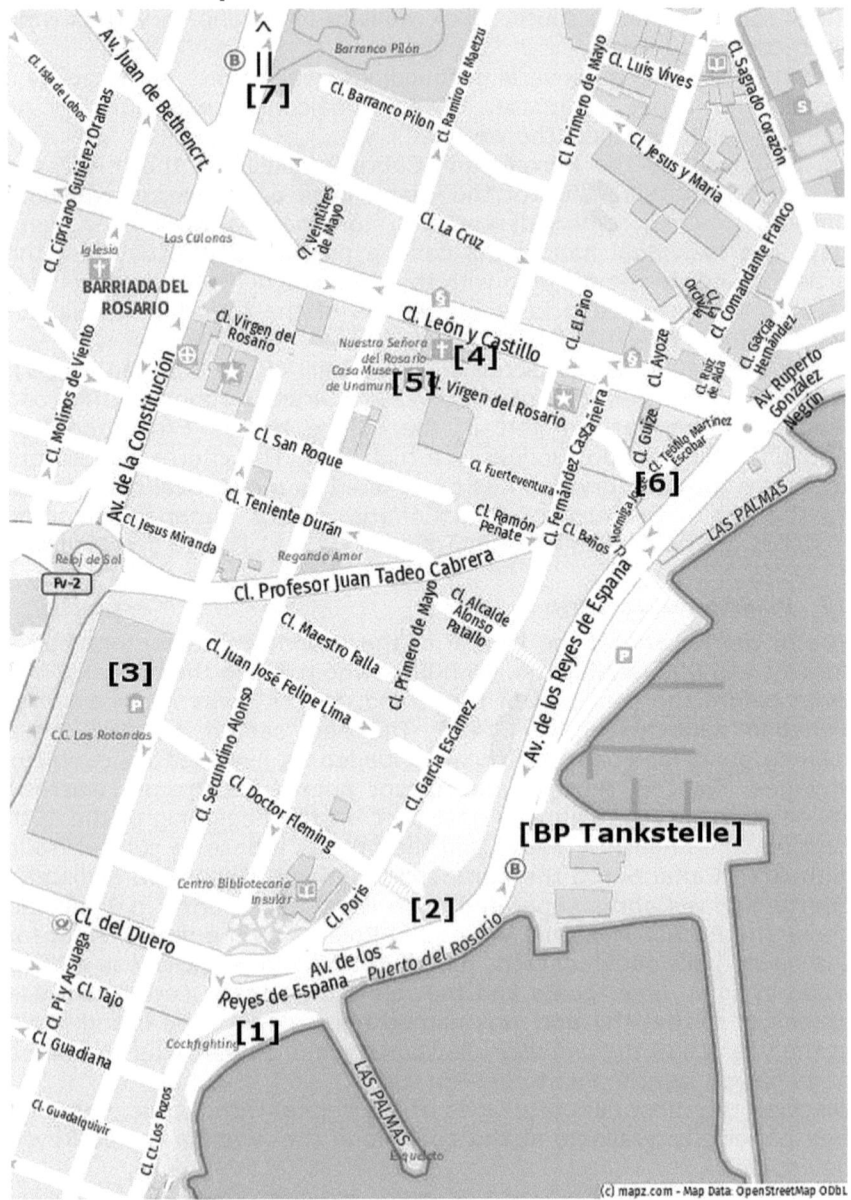

ATTENTION: BP Tankstelle = BP Petrol Station

Tour through the capital Puerto del Rosario
Discover the most beautiful sides of the capital. Best and free parking is available at the port along the Avenida de los Reyes de España. The BP filling station serves as a point of orientation.
If you follow the promenade to the left, you will arrive directly at the well-kept, fine sandy city beach **Playa Chica [1]**.
To get to the city centre, cross the crosswalk at the BP petrol station and then turn left. After the 2nd building on the right-hand side you will come to a small **square [2]** above the stairs leading up to the city centre Centro Ciudad. At the end you will pass Calle García Escámez and automatically come to Calle Dr. Flemming. Now there are 2 options: If you continue along the street, you will end up in Fuerteventura's largest shopping centre, the **Centro Comercial Las Rotondas [3]**.☉ Mon-Sat 10-20 o'clock, Sun closed
① All information about the current brand shops at: www.lasrotondascentrocomercial.com
If you take the first street to the right, it is Calle Primero Mayo, which was the pulsating artery of the capital before the shopping centre opened. Nearly all shops were closed and moved to the new center, so that in the cruise free time you will find an almost deserted pedestrian zone where only a few cafes are open.
Shortly before the end of the avenida, at the confluence of Calle Virgen del Rosario, there is the Cabildo, the city hall of the city, in front of which a souvenir pavilion with souvenirs typical for the island is placed.☉ Mon- Fr 10.15- 13.30, 17.30- 20
Behind it is the parish church of **Nuestra Señora del Rosario [4]**. It was built in 1812 and was the first religious building in the centre of the island. It was a small house of prayer dedicated to the Virgin El Rosario. In 1824- 1835 the central bell tower was added, which is now integrated into the eastern facade. The wrought-iron, decorated grilles on the main portal are striking. In the middle of the high altar is the patron saint of the church with the Child Jesus in her arms.
In the row of houses to the left of the church is the **Casa Museo Unamuno [5]**. In 1877 the building was entered in the land register of Puerto de Cabras, the original name of Puerto del Rosario.At that time it was a small guesthouse, which was run under the name "Hotel Fuerteventura". This is where the Spanish writer Miguel de Unamuno lived during his exile on the island. The museum is a testimony of typical architecture of canarian houses from that time.☉daily 9-14 pm, ♦free entrance, ①additional information: Miguel de Unamuno was professor and rector of the spanish university in Salamanca. Due to critical remarks against the regime he was banished to Fuerteventura by the then head of state on 12

March 1924. He lived 5 months in exile on the island, made friends with the inhabitants and wrote down his impressions of Fuerteventura, which were published in daily newspapers in Madrid, Buenos Aires and Gran Canaria. He then fled voluntarily to France to take up his fight against the dictatorship outside Spain. For his 100th birthday, the island government erected a monument to him on the Montaña Quemada, not far from the village of Tindaya.

In the city you can visit 2 weekly food markets:

Mercado Municipal [6]: If you follow Calle Primero de Mayo to the end, you will find Calle Léon y Catillo, which you follow to the right - towards the sea. Before the roundabout, turn right into Calle Teófilo Martínez Escobar and follow the street until you see the small market hall Mercado Municipal on your left. The traders offer a selection of fruit, vegetables, meat, fish and goat cheese. ☀ Mon-Fri 7-13 ⓘVisit this small market with the friendly sellers while it is still possible. Due to a low number of visitors, it could be foreseeable that this small market hall will not exist permanently.

Mercado Agrario de Fuerteventura [7]: At the end of Calle de Primero Mayo turn left into Calle Léon y Castillo, which you follow to the left. You will come to a roundabout and the main street Avenida La Constitución, which you follow to the right. In front of the 2nd roundabout, which leads to the right into Avenida Diego Miller, you will find the building of the central bus station Estación de Guaguas, where the market is located on the upper floor. Homemade products and regional food are offered. ☀ Sat 8-14

ⓘYou might also be interested in this: While strolling along the beach promenade you will encounter many sculptures by local artists. In the city centre, you can see graffiti art on old residential buildings. In January 2011, the planning office decided to have decaying building facades of the capital beautified. After consultation with the owners, the "Concurso de Arte Urbano de Puerto de Rosario", a competition for artistic design, was announced in 2015. In the meantime, more than 36 artists were allowed to realize their works on house walls. Due to positive feedback from islanders and tourists this project will be continued.

ⓘ Alternatively, park at the Centro Comercial Las Rotondas shopping centre.

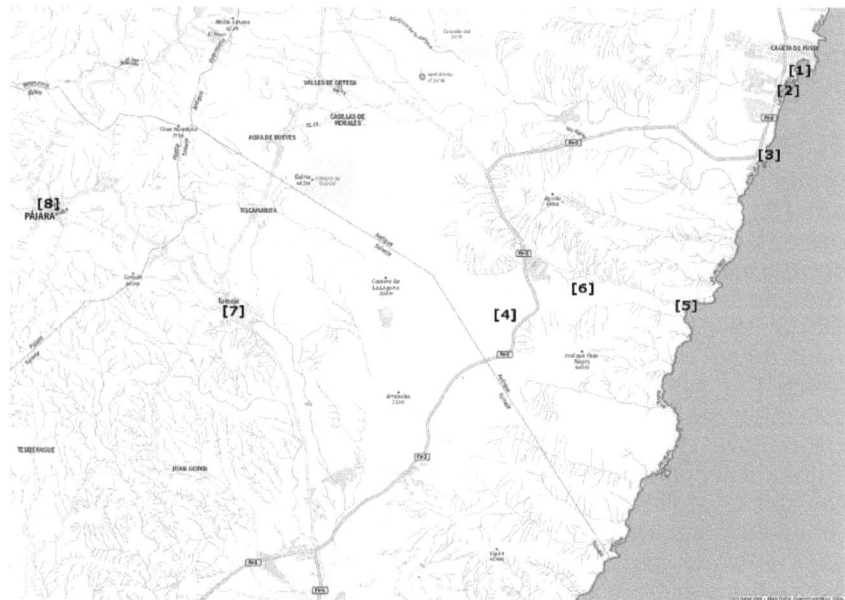

19 Caleta de Fueste

The village was created on the drawing board and consists of a collection of holiday resorts, hotels, small shopping centres and many restaurants. A long promenade leads directly along the big, artificially arranged snow-white main beach **Playa Caleta de Fuestes Beach [1].** Worth seeing is the fortified tower from the year 1740, which stands at the promenade in front of the Barceló-hotel complex. It is identical in construction with the Castillo de El Tostón in El Cotillo. These defence towers protected the coasts from the frequent attacks by pirates, English and French.

The popular Africa market is located on the main road FV-2 directly above the roundabout. ✪ Tue+ Sat 10-14

20 Playa La Guirra

South of Caleta de Fuestes is the holiday resort of Playa La Guirra, which includes Fuerteventura's first 18-hole golf course. Opposite, on the sea side, are spacious hotels and the shopping centre Centro Comercial Atlantico. ➀ www.ccatlanticofuerteventura.com

The promenade begins at the centre, where several **lime kilns [2]** from times gone by can be seen. From here you can walk to Caleta de Fuestes.

21 Salinas del Carmen

In the district of Salinas del Carmen is the salt museum **Museo de la Sal [3]**. The facility consists of 2 complexes. In the main building there is a permanent exhibition on the history of salt and the Salinas del Carmen salt works, built at the beginning of the 20th century. The tour begins to the left of the building complex.

Station 1- Saltadero: This is the highest point of the salt flats. The wind drives the waves to the rocks. On impact a foam is formed in which the salt concentration is highest. The water collects in the collecting basin and is passed on. Station 2- Cocederos: The collected water flows through a canal into further collecting basins. Station 3- Tajos: When the water has reached the Cocedero, it evaporates and the salt crystallizes. A thin film of salt forms on the surface, which is removed twice a day to allow the salt to settle at the bottom. As soon as the water has almost completely evaporated, the salt worker skims the salt from the bottom and lets it drip off at the sides. It is then collected and brought to the camp. Station 4- Almacen: This is where the salt workers' tools are kept, the cleaned and dried salt is stored and packed in bags. Station 5- Embarcadero loading station: From the small quay El Muellito the salt was loaded in wagons for shipment to the neighbouring islands. Station 6- Horno de Cal- Lime kilns: Lime was needed for the construction of the salt works and their maintenance. In the period from October to March, when no salt could be extracted, lime was burned in the kilns. The stone kiln has 2 chambers on the side to store limestone and burnt lime. Station 7- Aljibe- Cistern: The cistern is located in a small depression where water for the supply of the finca was collected.

◐ 01.11.-30.04. 9.30-17.30, 01.05-31.10. 10-18,♨ 6,00€, children 0-3 years free, 4-11 years 3,00€, ⌂ FV-2- between km 23 and 24

22 Grand Malpais

The coastal road between Pozo Negro and Gran Tarajal passes through the **Malpais Grande[4]**. It is a volcanic landscape, which is covered with large and small volcanic lumps. This region is so called because after strong eruptions of the volcanoes Caldera de La Laguna and Caldera de Liria the translated "big bad land" was difficult to pass for the natives. ⌂ FV-2

23 pozo negro

The small fishing village of **Pozo Negro[5] was one** of the most important ports on the island in the 15th century due to its natural harbour. In the meantime, it only attracts locals for bathing at the weekend and some tourists for eating in the two fish restaurants. ⌂ FV-2> FV- 420 > End of road

The main attraction of Pozo Negros is the open-air museum Centro de Interpretacion Poblado de **La Atalayita[6]**. A bumpy path leads to the now permanently closed interpretation centre, which is located half underground in the earth. On foot follow the sign Poblado de La Atalayita. The village is named after the elevated volcanic cone Lomo de Atalayita, which the natives used as a lookout post to monitor the coastal section of Pozo Negro. La Atalayita occupies an area of 45,000 square metres, on which 115 buildings with different structures are located. Essentially the life of the natives took place outdoors. They inhabited small circular buildings made of piled up lava stones. Some were used permanently for generations, others served as hiding places during raids by the conquerors. At the entrance of the village a building has been restored, which reflects the traditional architecture of the island and the local architecture. In contrast to the other buildings, the ground plan is rectangular. The roof consists of a rod and bar construction to which clay is applied. On the side of the house you can see shell remains of mussels and snails. They were the most important source of food after fish and were used as simple tools. Most of the dwellings have a diameter of 1.50 - 2.00 m, a circular or elliptical ground plan. The entrance is narrow and low. Furthermore, there are contiguous residential complexes with outbuildings that open up to a central square surrounded by walls. In further separated areas shepherd dogs, goats, sheep and camels were kept. The Majos also used lava caves as living space, which were accessed through narrow wall openings with steps. ☉ Daily, ▮ free, ⌂ FV-2 > FV- 420 km 3

24 Tuineje

In the centre of the village is the church **Iglesia San Miguel Arcangel [7]**. The inhabitants are proud of their successfully fought battle against the English on the volcanic mountain Tamasite in 1740, which was depicted on two panels on the right and left of the altar base.

The Battle of Tamasite: After the discovery of America, the Canary Islands became the most important stopover before the Atlantic crossing for the Spanish royal family. In the year 1730, the English royal house declared war on the Spanish in order to assert its claims in the Canarian Islands. However, it was not until 10 years later, on 12 October 1740, that 50 heavily armed English corsairs arrived in the port of Gran Tarajal to conquer the then capital, Betancuria. From Gran Tarajal they made good progress towards Tuineje through the dry gorges without being discovered. According to legend the English invaded the settlement Casillas Blanca south of Tamasite on October 13th. They forced a peasant to lead them to the commander in Betancuria. However, he was able to get one of his sons to run over the 346 m high mountain of Tamasite in time to alert the inhabitants of Tuineje. The church bells were immediately rung from village to village. When the English reached Tuineje they first plundered the church. They noticed that the inhabitants had lined up and help from the surrounding villages was approaching. Then they decided to retreat towards the sea. The commander of the natives asked for the help of the patron saint San Miguel and ordered the farmers to gather their dromedaries to face the English south of the Tamasite at the pass of El Cuchillo. The dromedaries intercepted the hail of bullets, so that the farmers emerged as victors from this battle. They made an oath to their patron saint, but this was forgotten in the course of time. About 200 years later, in 1946, the clergyman of Tuineje reminded the inhabitants of the historical battle. He set 13 October as a feast day, which is still celebrated today.

25 Pájara

Pájara is one of the oldest places on the island. It was founded by shepherds and fishermen who settled here in the 16th century.
The church **Iglesia Nuestra Señora de la Regla**I s worth seeing **[8]**. Construction began in 1645 and was completed in 1687. In the 18th century the church was extended by the right side nave. The striking stonemasonry work on the portal was created by local artists, who probably took ideas and inspiration from Italian model books. They are Aztec inspired and look like snakes, feathers, suns and lions. In front of the church there is a restored water well, a so-called Noria, which was once set in motion by camels. In the meantime it is only a tourist attraction, which is irregularly driven by a donkey.

☉ Daily 9-15 o'clock, ♨ switching on the church lights 6 min. 1,00€, ⌂ FV-30, Calle La Regla,8- 35628 Pájara > town centre

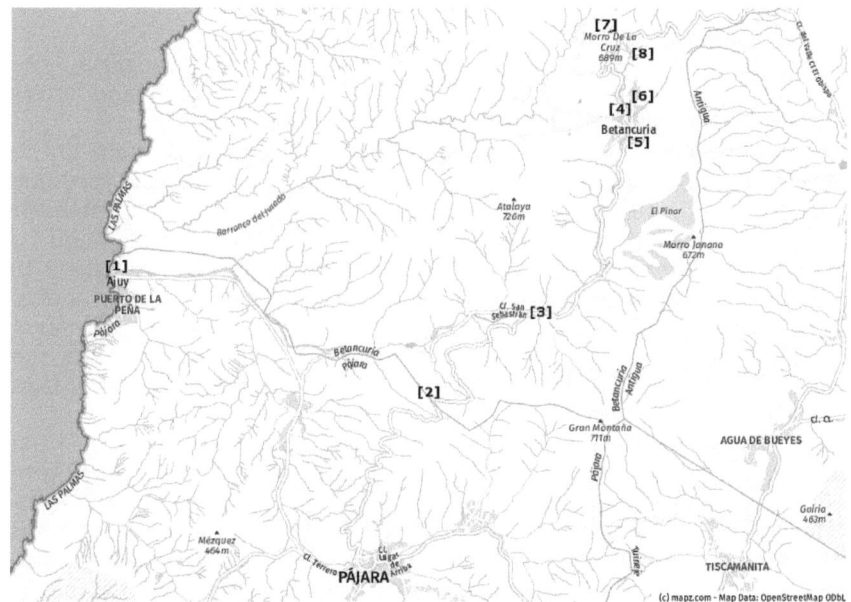

26 Ajuy

The FV-621 leads directly to the small fishing village of **Ajuy[1]**, which is also called Puerto de la Peña - port on the rocky coast. The 10 km long coastline was declared a Monumento Natural in 1994 because of its important history and the impressive limestone formations.

Between the cliffs you will find the beautiful, deep black sand beach Playa de Los Muertos- the beach of the dead. The name dates back to the time of conquest, when pirates went to this place and caused a cruel bloodbath among the inhabitants. You can sunbathe, but should not go swimming because of strong undercurrents.

On the right side of the beach a footpath leads to the highlights of the village. You walk along the rugged coast and after about 20 minutes you will see the first lime kilns. Here you can go down or follow the trail. You come to a viewing platform from which you can discover the large volcanic cave downhill over steps. In those days the inhabitants found refuge in the extensive branching tunnels during pirate attacks.❶ You can park at the designated parking lot above the fishing village, or continue to the 2nd parking lot directly on the beach. ⌂ FV- 621

27 Vega de Río Palmas

From Pájara the FV-30 leads in the direction of Betancuria. The winding route passes volcanic peaks up to 700 m high and offers fantastic views all the way to the sea.

Shortly after the road sign Degollada de los Granadillos there is the 1st observation deck Mirador del Risco de la Peña. As you continue your journey, you will come across the second viewpoint, **Mirador Las Peñitas[2]**, from which you can see a reservoir surrounded by palm trees. The community planned a large-scale reservoir here to use water for agriculture. Proliferating tamarisk plants on the shores made the water salty and led to the silting up of the lake. Environmentalists have been campaigning for the preservation of the trees, so that the reservoir can now only be recognised as a lake after heavy rainfall.

Once you arrive in the village, you have the possibility to drive to the beginning of the reservoir. ⌂ FV-30> at the end of the village turn left> Calle San Sebastián> after the Casa de la Naturaleza turn left> Calle Puerto de la Peña> follow the street to the end, Direct access ❶to the reservoir is not allowed due to a private barrier. Here cacti were planted for the cultivation of cochineal plants. On the leaves you can see a white layer of mould, under which the cochineals grow. The louse originally comes from Mexico and produces a red dye which is used to colour fabrics, food and also in cosmetics. In 1835, the louse was imported to Lanzarote and Fuerteventura. The offspring of the cacti are infected with the insect in spring. In summer, the adult thick aphids are scraped off with metal spoons, dried and cleaned according to traditional methods. With the artificial production of the red dye, breeding lost its importance. Due to the return to natural raw materials, the cochineal is currently experiencing a revival on the islands.

At the end of the village is the pilgrimage church of **Virgen de La Peña[3]**. It houses the patron saint of the island of Fuerteventura. In the centre of the main altar is the Nuestra Señora de la Peña- the Holy Virgin Mary. After the Virgen de Las Nieves in La Palma, it is the second oldest picture of the Virgin Mary in the Canary Islands. The only 23 cm high statue was made of alabaster and is framed by a silver sun and a golden crescent. It is believed that the conqueror Juan de Béthencourt brought the little Madonna from France to the island. It is said that the statue was found by a Franciscan friar from Betancuria on a nearby volcanic mountain and was taken to the Convento de San Buenaventura for safekeeping. When the pirate Xabán Arráez invaded Betancuria in order to destroy the town, the monks decided to hide the statue of the Madonna below the village. Years later it was discovered in a small cave and brought to the pilgrimage church.☉ Daily 10-15, ⌂ FV- 30

28 Betancuria

Betancuria is the largest natural park on the island with over 150 square kilometres and occupies 10% of the total area. The place was the capital of the island and has a long history: the French nobleman and knight Jean de Béthencourt had conquered Fuerteventura in the twinkling of an eye from Lanzarote by order of his king Henry III. He founded Betancuria as the first city in the entire archipelago and gave it his name. After the expulsion of the indigenous people, craftsmen and farmers were settled in the valley, which at that time was still rich in water. Thanks to their craftsmanship and their distinctive knowledge of agriculture and livestock breeding, the town developed rapidly. In 1593, North African pirates attacked Betancuria with the dreaded leader Xabán de Arráez Betancuria and almost completely razed it to the ground. But already in the same year the reconstruction work of the city began. At that time, many mansions shaped the appearance of the town. When in 1835 Puerto de Cabras, today's Puerto del Rosario, was declared the capital of the island, Betancuria lost its importance.

The church of **Santa Maria de Betancuria[4]** stands in the midst of mansions of former nobles and church members and modest dwellings of farmers and craftsmen. It dates back to 1410 and was commissioned by the conqueror Jean de Béthencourt. The building was intended to replace the oratory built after the conquest and to house the image of the Virgin brought by the conquerors. This is also where the indigenous people who survived the conquest were christianized. After the pirate attack in 1593 the church and other buildings of the village burned down. The residents soon began the restoration. Under the final direction of the master builder Pedro de Párraga, the reconstruction of the church lasted until the end of the 17th century. More than a century of construction work left a mixture of Gothic, Renaissance, Baroque and Mudejar styles.
The church of Betancuria was the seat of the cathedral chapter. It stands out from the other churches on the island due to its size and its wealth of building materials. The church consists of 3 naves separated by semicircular stone arches. The wooden ceilings are in Mudejar style and the square tower is attached to the epistle wall with semi-circular and pointed arches. The façade is in Renaissance

style. It is carved in white stone and has a broken pediment. The columns decorated with vases and plant motifs are particularly noteworthy. After the entrance portal you will see a gilded altar from the 17th century, decorated with multicoloured plant motifs. It is the work of the sculptor Francisco Hernández. In the centre is the Nuestra Señora de la Concepción- the virgin of the conception from the 18th century. In the surrounding niches it is surrounded by the statues of San Antonio de Padua- Saint Anthony of Padua and San Pedro- Saint Peter. There are also 7 other altarpieces, of which the Baroque altar of the Inmaculata Concepción- the Virgin of the Immaculate Conception stands out. The rest of the sculptural inventory is made up of images that reflect Franciscan piety. You will also find a picture of the soul, a pulpit with the apostles and elements of the Eucharist, similar to those found in other churches in Fuerteventura, and a carved multi-coloured wooden choir.

The visit of the church ends in the sacristy in which the Museum of Sacred Art - Museo de Arte Sacro is located. Here the richly decorated Mudejar coffered ceiling attracts all eyes. It is divided into small boxes and decorated with multicoloured rosettes and gilded plant elements. Canvases from the 17th century hang on the walls. They depict scenes from the lives of the Virgin Mary and Jesus. Another painting by the tenerifenic painter Nicolás Medina from the year 1730 shows the nave.

☉ Mon-Sat 10- 12.30/13-15.50, Sun 10.30-14.20, ▌ 1,50 €, ⌂ Plaza Santa Maria de Betancuria,1- 35637 Betancuria

In the building complex in front of the church there is a big souvenir shop with countless articles. Beside it there is the Centro Insular de Artesanía. In the inner courtyard you walk through a small ethnological exhibition, where you get an impression of the life, work and creativity of the indigenous people. The visit includes a 3D film about the underwater world of the island. Through the garden you can reach the café-restaurant with an outside terrace. ☉ Daily 10 - 16 o'clock, ▌6,00 €,① You can enter the café without entrance through the back of the building. ⌂ Plaza Concepción, 11- 35637 Betancuria

The newly built **Museo Arqueologico Insular** is located on the main road FV-30 **[5]**.① Upon request to the official responsible body the opening of the archaeological island museum will take place this year. The date was not yet known at the time of printing, ⌂FV-30-km 17, Calle Amador Rodriguez-35637 Betancuria

At the exit sign of Betancuria- direction Mirador de Morro Velosa - a concrete road goes downhill on the right. It leads to the ruins of the monastery church **Convento de San Buenaventura [6]**. Shortly after the Spanish crown conquered the island, the construction of the first Franciscan monastery in the Canary Islands began here in 1416. The missionaries had the task to Christianize the pagan natives. At the left entrance side of the building you will see a small marble plaque. This dates back to one of the Spanish conquerors named Diego García de Herrera. He chose Fuerteventura as the starting point for his slave trade and was buried in the monastery in 1485. Opposite the ruins of the monastery you will reach the hermitage of San Diego through a small opening in the wall. It was built in the second half of the seventeenth century and is permanently closed. According to tradition, it was built on the site of a small cave where Saint Diego prayed during his stay in Betancuria between 1441 and 1449. San Diego de Alcalá was assigned to the Canary Islands in 1441, and five years later took the office of abbot. There he dedicated himself to the Christianization of the natives and defended them from the rapacity of the Spanish conquerors. This caused him many problems so that he was forced to return to Spain in 1449. ⌂ FV-30

On the way to the Mirador de Morro Velosa, you will find the **Mirador de Guise y Ayose[7]**. The FV-30 divides the viewpoint, which is located between Betancuria on the right and the Valle Santa Inés on the left. Until the arrival of the conquerors, Fuerteventura was divided into two kingdoms: Maxorata in the north and Jandía in the south. The impressive 4.50m high statues present Guise, the king of Maxorata and Ayose, the king of Jandía. Without bloody battles against the conquerors, they surrendered to their enemies without fighting and allowed themselves to be Christianized. The baptisms took place on 18 and 28 January 1405, with which they received the new names Luis and Alfonso. ⌂ FV-30

29 Mirador de Morro Velosa

If you continue on the FV-30 you will come to the 645 m high volcanic mountain Tegú with the viewpoint **Mirador de Morro Velosa[8]**. It was designed by the Lanzarote artist César Manrique (1919-1992) in the style of a Canarian mansion and was completed in 1997.❶ Upon request to the official responsible body, the Mirador was closed for renovation work on 17.05.2019. Already in 2011 the Morro Velosa was renovated. The activities that were scheduled for 6 months at that time ultimately lasted 20 months.

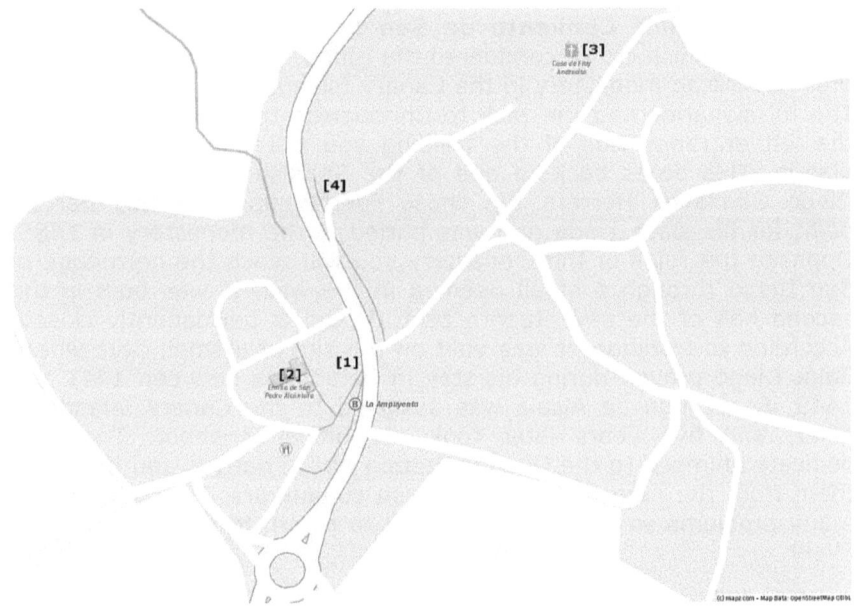

30 La Ampuyenta

This sleepy village is located on the FV-20, km-15 between Casillas de Angel and Antigua.

On the main thoroughfare there is a complex of buildings consisting of three interconnected houses. The building was built as a hospital-hospital San Conrado y San Gaspar, but was never used as such. At the moment it houses the tourist information. On the backside free guided tours to the attractions of the village start. You will see the Ermita de San Pedro de Alcantara, the birthplace of Frailito Andrés, the Casa Museo Doctor Mena and the hospital.◐ Tue- Sa 10.30/ 12.30/ 14.30 +16.00,◑ To ensure the execution of the tour, please contact, or your hotel reception please call 928 85 89 98 (Mon-Fri 8-15 o'clock). If the guided tour does not take place, you can start a small tour of La Ampuyenta on your own: At the back of the **Hospital San Conrado y San Gaspar [1]** you will directly meet the **Ermita de San Pedro de Alcantara[2]**. The small church was founded in 1681 by Don Pedro Medina and his wife Doña Agustina de Bethancourt. It is surrounded by a crenellated wall. The façade has a round-arched portal, above which a round decorative oculus window lets diffuse light into the building. Inside there is an important collection of paintings, murals and easels dating from the second half of the 18th century. The mural paintings in the chapel are considered to be one of the most important preserved in the Canary Islands, where painting, architecture and sculpture blend together. The important legacy of San Pedro de Alcántara de La Ampuyenta includes 16 different paintings, most of which allegorically depict the figure of San Pedro- Saint Peter, as well as a high altarpiece, several sculptures and the saint's walks. The devotion reached its peak with his canonisation in 1669.

You return to the hospital, go through the traffic lights and turn into the opposite street Camino Ampuyenta. Past a ruin typical of the island on the left-hand side, follow the road. You come to a small roundabout with the bust of Fray Andresito and continue straight on. Next to house no. 15b is the **Casa de Fray Andresito[3]**. The house is a small and simple sanctuary in honour of the Franciscan friar Andrés Filomeno García Acosta. He was also known as Fray Andresito- brother Andresito or Frailito Andrés and was born in Ampuyenta in 1800. He lived there with his brothers Eugenio and Maria until 1833, when he emigrated to Chile via Uruguay. In Montevideo he joined the Franciscan Order and moved to the capital Santiago de Chile. He died in 1853 and Fray Andresito is known as an apostle of the poor and is considered one of the most respected persons in the ecclesial world for his merciful deeds. The building was donated to the island government, which restored it in every detail. In the centre is the altarpiece under which the faithful leave offerings and donations. ☉ Every day.

When you return to the main road and go down to the right you will find **Casa Museo Doctor Mena[4]**. Tomás Antonio de San Pedro Mena Mesa, better known in Fuerteventura as Doctor Mena, was born in La Ampuyenta on 20 February 1802 in a very modest family without financial means and was baptised on 12 March in the parish church of Santa Ana in Casillas del Ángel, after only a few weeks. His parents, José León Mena Medina and María de San Diego Mesa y Carrión, had to sell 10 bushels of barley to send him to Las Palmas to study, since there were no schools or teachers in the community.

After completing his undergraduate studies, he began his studies, which he passed with distinction on 19 February 1820 and was awarded a chair of philosophy. Dr. Mena resigned from this chair when he was called by his brother Conrado, who was a priest in Havana and had a certain fortune. It is said that he arrived at Havana harbor with nothing but his luggage, a shirt and a handkerchief. He began his university studies in Cuba, but first had to present his family tree, which showed that he had no mixture or race of Moors, Jews, heretics or prisoners among his ancestors. To identify him, he presented as witnesses Francisco Bueno and José Sicilia, natives of Fuerteventura, who declared that he was the son of José León Mena and María de San Diego Mesa, natives of Casillas del Ángel. After the legitimacy was confirmed, he began his medical studies.

On 27 March 1825 he was awarded the degrees of Bachelor of Medicine and Bachelor of Surgery. Convinced that he had much to learn, he set off for Paris, visiting hospitals and immersed himself in his studies. The stay in Paris lasted six years and provided him with extensive medical knowledge. After this time he returned to Havana, where he opened his practice and assisted in several epidemics of yellow fever and cholera. He proved to be an excellent doctor and capable surgeon. On 1 July 1846 he was appointed an academic of the Faculty of Medicine and Surgery of Cádiz.

At the age of 45 he returned to Fuerteventura, accompanied by his servant, to spend the rest of his life with his mother, who was widowed for the second time and continued to live in his birthplace.

For the rest of his days he decided to live a quiet life far away from the noise of the big cities. However, he could not, as he had wished, break away from his profession as a doctor. He felt obliged to treat the sick free of charge in his practice.

Dr. Mena often traveled to Tenerife, where he had many friends. He had a summer house in Los Rodeos (La Laguna), a rustic finca in Guamasa and another one in El Tornero (Tegueste). In Fuerteventura he owned properties in Casillas del Ángel, Tefía, Los Llanos and Ampuyenta, Betancuria, in the Santa Inés Valley, La Antigua, Vega de Tetir, Valle de Jaifas in La Oliva, Costa de Los Lajares and Puerto Cabras.

He built a two-storey solitary house in El Buen Lugar, very close to the Barranco de Los Molinos, where he spent weeks surrounded by his books published in French on his return from Tenerife. In this house he kept the library and the surgical instruments, which he later bequeathed in his will to his partner and friend Don Bernardo Espinosa.

Doctor Mena's extensive library was burned by his relatives after his death to roast wheat and corn.

After the death of his mother, he suffered from a heart disease, so he decided to move to Tenerife, to the residence of Mrs. Antonia Rodríguez Núñez, who took care of him until his death on July 10, 1868, at the age of 66. The house in La Ampuyenta, where he spent the last years of his life, was converted into the Casa Museo Doctor Mena in his honour.

In his will of 26 July 1864, written four years before his death, Dr. Mena left an inheritance of 25,000 pesetas for the construction of a hospital, now known as the "Hospitalito de la Ampuyenta".

Molino [7]

Molina[8]

Space for personal notes...✎...

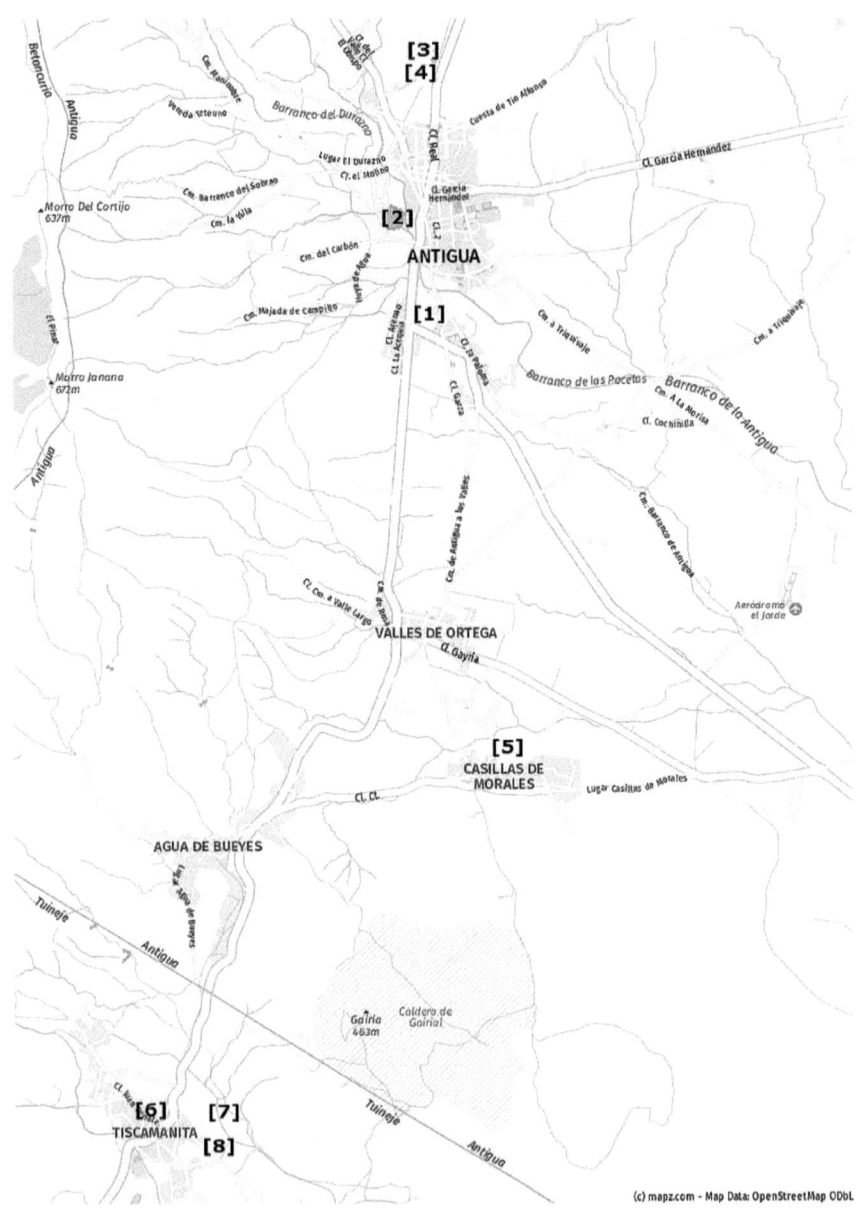

31 Antigua

La Antigua is one of the first villages to be established in Fuerteventura. The foundation dates back to the second half of the 15th century, when French Norman and Andalusian families settled after the conquest. They used the fertile soil for agriculture and ran cattle breeding. Only on 07 October 1462 Pope Pius II abolished the captivity and slavery of the Canarian natives. From that moment on the first Marian images arrived in the Canary Islands.

The name La Antigua is most probably due to the desire of the first settlers to honour the Blessed Virgin, as this invocation was very common in both Andalusia and Castile. According to records, a hermitage dedicated to the Virgin of Antigua already existed in the village of Antigua around 1550. This chapel was extended and redesigned until it reached the current state of the church of Nuestra Señora de La Antigua.

From the middle of the 16th century, La Antigua tried to free itself from the religious and political centralism of Betancuriana.

Betancuria fought against anything that could have jeopardized its status as capital, since the feudal lords knew that La Antigua had the most fertile areas with greater economic development and demographic growth.

The religious decay of the historic Villa de Betancuria was reached on 11 September 1785, when the parish church of Nuestra Señora de La Antigua was consecrated.

In 1812 Antigua was founded as an independent municipality, a process that began in 1808. In 1834 Antigua became the capital of the island. This led to a bitter confrontation between Diego del Castillo Zeruto, the Mayor of Antigua, and Ambrosio Bethencourt Robles, the Mayor of Betancuria, who refused to transfer the archives of the "Notarial Protocols of Fuerteventura" to the new capital of the island. Demonstrations were taking place at that time, including armed captivity, which forced the militias to enforce order. Finally, in 1850, by order of the Royal Audience of the Canary Islands, the archive was deposited in the Antigua Town Hall until it was handed over to the Canarian Museum for safekeeping in 1930. But in the year 1860, La Antigua lost its importance completely when the Puerto de Cabras of that time, the current Puerto del Rosario, was declared the seat of government.

At the entrance of the village, coming from Tiscamanita, a stately, pastel-coloured **mansion [1]** in colonial style bears witness to Antigua's former importance and wealth. ⌂ FV-20, km-20. Worth seeing is the church **Nuestra Señora de la Antigua[2]**, inaugurated in 1785.☉ daily, ⌂ Calle Plaza3, 35630 Antigua

One of the biggest attractions is the windmill **Molino de Antigua[3]** with the cheese museum **Museo de Queso Majorero- MQM [4].**

The history of goat breeding and cheese in Fuerteventura began with the first settlers of the island and goes back to the first century AD.

Already in 1403 the Norman conquerors praised the delicacies of goat's cheese. A contemporary chronicler wrote: "They are well supplied with cheese, which is extremely good, the best known in these regions, is made only from goat's milk, of which the whole country is full, more than on any other island; and every year you could take 60,000 goats and use their leather and fat, each animal of which brings much, ... at least 30 or 40 pounds".

More than 2,000 years after these beginnings the MQM- Museo del Queso Majorero was planned and carried out. The main attraction is the restored 17th century windmill of Antigua. The entrance is on the left side of the building. On an area of 500 sqm you will find 3 showrooms with interesting information about Fuerteventura. In addition to geology, fauna and flora, the goat and Majorero cheese are the subject of a detailed discussion in the second exhibition room: The Majorera goat breed, the relationship with the natural environment, sheep farming, milking and morphology. The third exhibition is dedicated to history and culture: traditional production, traditional trade, characteristics of Majorero cheese, Canary Island cheeses, Designation of Origin, nutritional aspects and recipes.◑ In the adjoining courtyard with souvenir shop you can taste the cheeses. Don't miss to make a detour to the cactus garden of the plant, which is a little bit hidden, left behind the entrance. ☉ Tue- Fr 9.30- 17.30, ♨ 2,00 €, ⌂ FV-20, km19

32 Valles de Ortega

Only 4 km south of Antigua, on the FV-20, is the small village of Valles de Ortega, which shares the Ermita de San Roque with the neighbouring community of Casillas de Morales.☉ Open during trade fairs, ⌂Barrio Goma 31, 35638 Antigua. The church was donated in 1732 after a long plague epidemic by farmers from the region. Beautiful photo motives offer the ruins in **Casillas de Morales [5]**, which you see directly on the field next to the main road.

33 Tiscamanita

The most prominent point of Tiscamanita is an old restored windmill, which houses the **Interpretation Centre of Molinos [6]**. You will explore the premises of a miller's family and can visit the gofio mill.☻ Tue-Sat 10- 17.30, 🕯2,00 €, At the① entrance you will receive a brochure with explanations about grinding tools like mortars, hand mills, millstones, the grinding process and the production of gofio. ⌂ Calle La Cruz 11, 35683 Tiscamanita

Windmills- Molino or Molina?
Windmill translated into Spanish is Molino, but windmill is not equal to windmill.
The conquest and colonisation of Fuerteventura brought about a radical change in the way of life of its inhabitants, who moved from a nomadic life to a sedentary life and to a predominantly agricultural economic model with cereal cultivation. Population growth led to the introduction of new production systems for the manufacture of basic products such as gofio and flour.
First the so-called "blood mills" were used, in which animals and humans were responsible for crushing the grain. Later, the forces of nature were used for this hard work, which led to a considerable increase in the production of these basic products.
Windmills were introduced in Fuerteventura between the end of the 18th and the beginning of the 19th century, at a time when the cultivation of tomatoes, fodder crops, wheat and barley flourished. Its foundation was favoured by the presence of the trade winds. For this reason, they were built in wind-open places, especially in the north and centre of the island, where they shaped the rural landscape. The windmills gradually led to the abandonment of other more traditional methods of grain milling, such as the Tahona or hand mill, which were found in almost every house. Although they did not disappear completely, they were still used at home and in times of calm.
There are two types of windmills: The **Molino[7]** and the **Molina[8]**.
El Molino: The traditional windmill is known on the island as the "men's mill". It was the first to arrive in Fuerteventura and is a copy of the mills of Castile. They are circular and have two to three storeys and four to six windmill blades. The joints of the masonry are made of clay or white lime mortar. The mill consists of two millstones, the funnel and the chute, which are located at the foot of the tower. Under the conical wooden roof is the gear wheel with its axis, the press screw and the windmill blades, which are anchored on a slightly inclined horizontal axis. The alignment of the blade rotor to the prevailing winds is achieved by means of a wooden shaft or

rudder located at the opposite end of the blade rotor, which allows the slanted and movable wooden deck to rotate through 360º.

La Molina: In the second half of the 19th century a new windmill was built on the island of La Palma, which was named Ortega System in honour of its inventor Isidoro Ortega Sánchez. It is the forerunner of the Molino windmill, known as Molina in Fuerteventura and Lanzarote. The Molinas come from variations made by local carpenters and craftsmen. They work similar to Molinos, but have simpler machines and a different appearance. The wind turbine is located on a single-storey building. The wooden tower carried the entire mechanism and was supported by a metal pin that rotated on an iron plate lying on the floor. The grinding mechanism consisted of two millstones, the funnel and the channel. The building consisted of a brick room with a rectangular floor plan in which the miller did his work. This had the advantage that he did not have to walk up and down the stairs with the heavy bags of grain.

The following mills on the island of Fuerteventura have been declared Heritage Sites:

La Oliva: Molino de Corralejo, Molina de Manolo Hierro, Molino de Domingo Estévez, Molina de Juan Morera, the Molinos de Villaverde, Molino del Roque, Molino de Lajares, Molina de Lajares, Molina Tindaya-Tebeto.

Puerto del Rosario: Molino de Tefía, die Molinos de Los Llanos de La Concepción, Molina de La Asomada, Molina de Puerto Lajas und die Molinas de Almácigo.

La Antigua: Molino de Antigua, Molinos de Valles de Ortega, Molina de Valles de Ortega, Molino de La Antigua-Durazno and Molino de La Corte. Tuineje: Molino de Tiscamanita.

①Explore the historic mills, most of which have been restored, and those that are also remote and subject to decay. In the village of Pajara, in front of the church there is an old water wheel - a Tahona, which is driven by a donkey when tourists are present.

Space for personal notes...✐...

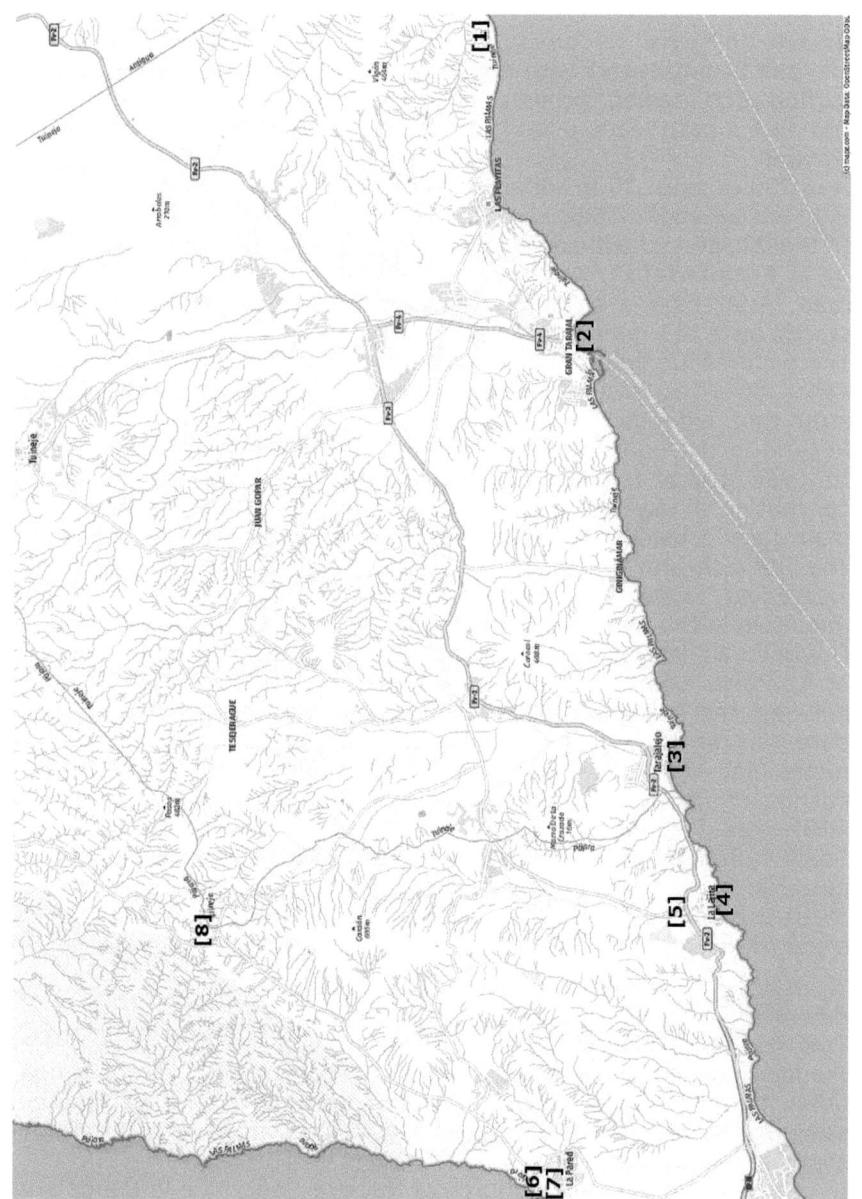

34 Las Playitas

Next to the small, picturesque fishing village Las Playitas, the huge Playitas Grand Resort with golf and tennis courts, as well as diving, surfing and sailing schools has been established. At the hotel complex a path leads directly to the dark sandy beach Playa de Las Playitas.

It is 700 m long, 30 m wide and in places it is covered with gravel. ⌂ Urb. Puerto Azul- 35629 Las Playitas

In the village you will come to the signposted lighthouse **Faro Punta de la Entallada[1]**, which you reach after about 6 km on an asphalt road. After only a short drive you will discover the tower, which stands on a 185 m high volcanic mountain.

The picturesque lighthouse is only about 48 miles from Cape Jubi off Africa. It is responsible for signalling the east coast, on the coastal strip that extends from the lighthouse in the capital Puerto del Rosario in the north and the lighthouse of Morro Jable in the south. In 1954 it was the last lighthouse built in Spain with the classic concept of a tower and a house for the lighthouse keeper. In the main façade black volcanic stones were covered with white plaster. The reddish-brown stones on the edges of the buildings and protruding ledges and plinths come from the Bermeja volcanic mountain in the municipality of Tefía.

Designed as early as 1921, it provided for the installation of a beacon at Lantaílla point to guide navigation in the narrowest passage between the African coast and the Canary Islands. What was finally built was an aircraft headlight with a glass dome above the 11-metre-high lighthouse, which emits its characteristic 1 and 2 white flashes of light every 18 seconds at 30 miles for ships and 15 kilometres for aircraft, which then form the route between the Spanish Sahara and Gando Airport in Gran Canaria.🕐 daily. It is not possible to visit the interiors, in🕐 front of the lighthouse you can reach a magnificent viewpoint via a wooden ramp. ⌂ on the FV-511, signposted.

35 Gran Tarajal

The FV-4 leads along a long palm tree avenue to Gran Tarajal. Here the locals benefit from the city's good infrastructure. It offers, among other things, a post office, a police headquarters, a central bus station, schools, sports grounds, a wrestling arena, and numerous shops and restaurants.

In the centre is the parish church of Nuestra Señora de la Candelaria. It was built in 1900 thanks to a generous donation from Don Matías

López, a Canary who emigrated to Cuba and who also contributed to the expansion of the port. Open for Mass☉,① Every year at the end of January, festivities are held in honour of the saint Señora de la Candelaria, ⌂Calle Juan Carlos,1- Plaza de La Candelaria

On the opposite square Plaza Alcalde Francisco De Léon García, under shady laurel trees, is a beautiful fountain with stone seahorses. The dark brown sandy beach **Playa de Gran Tarajal**extends in front of the long promenade **[2]**. It is 500 m long, 100 m wide and also suitable for children for bathing.

At the end of the village is the marina, the front part of which is decorated with a whale skeleton.

36 Tarajalejo

Tarajalejo is a place with seafaring traditions, which was founded as a fishing village under the protection of the mountainside. In the meantime many apartments and a hotel complex have settled here. In front of the promenade is the Playa de Tarajalejo, a fine dark sandy beach with pebbles and gravel. It is almost 1.5 km long and 45 m wide.

At the beginning of the 16th century the pier was an export point for animals shipped from Fuerteventura to Gran Canaria. From the 17th to the 18th century the port of Tarajalejo became the fourth most important pier in Fuerteventura and the second most important in the south of the island. Although it was one of the busiest ports in the south of the island, it had no fortifications to ward off possible pirate attacks.

A wide wooden bridge leads over a barranco, which in case of heavy rainfall drains the rainwater into the sea and divides the village into 2 parts.

In order to lend the waterfront a new splendour, five impressive sculptures were erected in November 2017. They represent "the sea and all that it represents and conveys". The ensemble of the **Mareseum** open-air museum **[3]** is explained on display boards. ⌂FV-2, in front of the Hotel R2 Bahia Playa Design Hotel& SPA, Avenida las Palmeras,28- 35627 Tarajalejo

37 La Lajita

Past dark brown volcanic mountains and small bays with black lava beaches, the FV-2 leads to La Lajita, a small nest of new buildings. The dark stone beach **Playa de La Lajita[4]** is mainly used by locals. On the beach there are picturesque little boats with which the fishermen go out to sea. The Ermita de la Inmaculada, which is only open during fair times, is located directly near the beach.☉ Sat 17-19, ⌂ Calle Tajinaste,1- 35627 La Lajita

The real highlight of the place is the Park **Oasis Wildlife Fuerteventura[5]**. It is the second largest zoo in the Canary Islands after Loro Park in Tenerife. On an area of 800,000 square meters more than 3,000 animals from 230 species, as well as the largest cactus garden in Europe can be visited. In the beautifully designed grounds you will meet, among others, various species of monkeys, flamingos, meerkats, crocodiles, otters, lynxes, giraffes, hippos, cheetahs, coatis, deer, camels, elephants, llamas, zebras, gazelles, emus and pelicans. In addition, 4 live shows take place several times a day: Parrot, sea lion, reptile and the birds of prey show.

➊You can travel individually or free of charge by Oasis Park buses from all resorts on the island. Due to the size of the complex, you should plan a whole day for this excursion. In order to see all live shows, it is advisable to build the visit around the shows. Because the ways are very long, you still don't manage to see almost all the shows. Parrots: 9.45/10.45/11.45/12.45, sea lions: 11.15/15.45, reptiles: 12.00/14.00, birds of prey: 13.15/15.00 Attractions with costs: Camel Safari, Sea Lion Experience- swimming with sea lions and Lemur Experience- body contact with monkeys. To do this, you will have to buy the tickets at the box office. Child friendly: Many playgrounds, at the main attractions you can buy food bags for the animals. Rental hand trucks make the long distances easier.

Transfer times and prices are available at the hotel reception or at www.oasiswildlifefuerteventura.com ⌂ FV-2, km 58

Every Sunday the well visited and worth seeing farmers and craftsmen market takes place in the entrance area of the Oasis Wildlife Fuerteventura Park. Only handmade products and local food are offered by local artists and producers.☉ Sun 9-13, ⌂ FV-2, km 58

38 La Pared

La Pared is located on the northwest coast of Jandía. The name is due to a stone wall that ran from the east to the west coast at the narrowest point of the island, the Istmo de la Pared. It is one of the most important archaeological sites of Fuerteventura. The wall was first mentioned in the 15th century during the Norman conquest. It is a pre-Hispanic construction on the isthmus that connected the Jandia peninsula with the rest of the island. Only a few sections of the 6 km long stone wall are now left, which have a height of 80 cm and a width of 50 cm. The missing stones were used at that time by the first settlers to build houses.

Before the island conquest, Fuerteventura was divided into the kingdoms of Maxorata and Jandía. King Guise ruled the north of the island and his brother King Ayose the south. The two kings rarely lived in harmony and separated their dominions by this wall. ① At the FV-30, between Betancuraia and La Antigua, the oversized, 4.50m high statues of the kings were staged at the Mirador de Guise y Ayose. To this day the same enmity exists between the Majoreros and the shepherds of the Jandia peninsula. In practice, the wall remains, as some goats skip the established boundaries and are immediately caught by their neighbour.

In the 1970s the plan of the island government to transform the coastal area of La Pared into an exclusive tourist enclave failed. In the meantime you will find here German residents with beautiful houses.

On the coast you will find two beautiful bays. **Playa del Viejo Rey[6]** is surrounded by cliffs and gives the 800 m long and 20 m wide sandy beach a wild character. Without a doubt this section is one of the most beautiful of the northwest coast. Surfers from the nearby surf schools get their money's worth here. ① The beach can be reached by stairs, ⌂FV-605, Calle Valle Ancho, straight on through the roundabout - Avenida del Istmo - to the end

From the top of the hill you can see the Playa de La Pared with the unique rock gate **Mirador La Pared[7]**. The short beach section is not suitable for swimming due to extremely strong undercurrents. Nevertheless, the small meerkats want to be fed along the rocky beach formation. ⌂FV-605, Calle Valle Ancho, turn right at the roundabout - direction Restaurante Bahia Pared

39   Mirador Astronómico de Sicasumbre

The **Mirador Astronómico de Sicasumbre[8]** is located on the route between La Pared and Pájara and was the first mirador on the island of Fuerteventura. It is designed to watch the night sky, but also offers beautiful views during the day. You will see the natural monument of Montaña Cardón, the Jandía Natural Park, as well as Montaña Hendida and the Degollada del Viento. The path to the lookout point is relatively well developed, halfway there is a small resting place with a wooden pergola. A little further on you will see an oxidized sign with the inscription "Fuerteventura", in front of which there are two goat sculptures. They are the work of the island sculptor Juan Miguel Cubas. You will also encounter interactive elements, such as a scale model of the solar system, to observe and identify the planets in the sky at night. A skyline to see the solstices and equinoxes completes the Mirador. Every year Fuerteventura celebrates the World Night of the Stars on 20th April. This day would be a good time to make a night excursion to the Astronomical Viewpoint of Sicasumbre and share the nocturnal experience of stargazing with other visitors and professionals.⏻ Parking facilities on the hard shoulder. The ascent takes about 20 minutes. ⌂FV- 605, between km 11 and 12

Space for personal notes...✎...

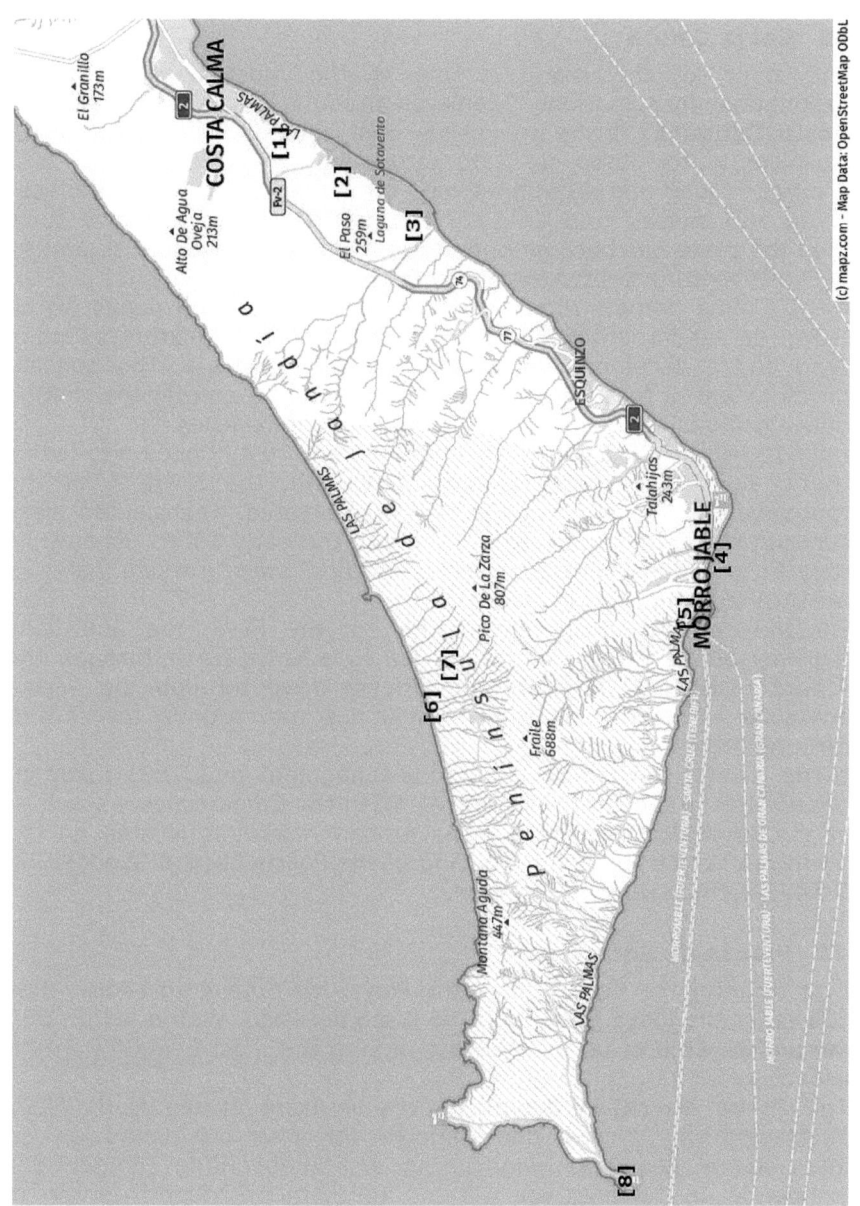

51

40   Costa Calma

The south of the island is one of the most popular holiday destinations for Canarians, Spaniards and foreigners. The coastline of **Costa Calma[1]** forms a wide bay that extends from Punta de los Molinillos to the Risco del Gato settlement, with a beach that is 2 kilometres long and 40 metres wide on average, and in some places up to 300 metres long. In 1977 the first hotel was built and since then the place has become one of the most important tourist centres in Fuerteventura, visited mainly by Germans.

Costa Calma borders directly on the snow-white sand dunes of the Istmo de Jandía isthmus, whose composition is a mixture of white sand and a decomposition of the volcanic substrate. The building development at that time reached into the dunes, so that the shifting dunes could not carry the beautiful sand to the beaches.

Until 2014, the FV-2 motorway ended before Costa Calma and led all traffic along an avenue of palm trees into the town. After the roundabout a laterally wooded park was created. The planted trees come from Australia and were planted in the early 1980s. Meanwhile they form a dense grove, which is irrigated with brackish water, a mixture of salt and fresh water.

For the current further construction of the FV-2, the multi-lane highway above Costa Calma was led in a large curve through the nature reserve. Hardly any car drivers drive through the village anymore, so that a peaceful silence has returned on the former through road.

①The lively town has numerous shopping and entertainment possibilities in the shopping centres - Centros Comerciales, as well as in the surroundings. The popular African market is located on the premises behind the police building of the Policia Local.◎ Wed + Sun 9-14, ⌂Avenida Happag Lloyd.

41   Playas de Sotavento

Directly after the Costa Calma the Playas de Sotavento begin. They consist of the Playa Barca and the Risco del Paso. With a length of 9 km and a width of 60 m, they are among the most beautiful on the island.

The **Playa Barca[2]** begins directly in front of the Hotel Melía Fuerteventura. It has been known for over 30 years as an international venue for windsurfing and kiteboarding competitions worldwide. In this area you will find René Egli's Surfsport Center. In the shallow, tidal lagoon, both beginners and pros will get their money's worth. Despite a section with sunbeds and umbrellas in front

of the center, the beach is not suitable for swimming. ⌂ FV-2, exit
Costa Calma, at the roundabout follow the signs to Melía
Fuerteventura

Directly after the Playa Barca follows the beach section **Risco del
Paso [3]**. It is another hotspot for wind and kitesurfing fans. ⌂ FV-2,
direction Morro Jable- signposted

Playa del Mal Nombre is the last beach in the area of the Playas de
Sotavento. ➀ Round stone walls on the beach serve as wind
protection. A beach restaurant is available, ⌂ FV-2, direction Morro
Jable- exit 77 times Nombre. Following the signs, you will find an
abandoned hotel at the lower roundabout, behind which an
unfinished track leads to the beach on the left.

42 Jandía Playa

Before the almost endless, spectacular Playa de Jandía begins, you
will encounter the bays of Playa de Esquinzo and Playa de Butihondo.
They lie below rock walls and become relatively narrow at high tide.
The beach Playa de Esquinzo has a length of approximately 3 km and
is divided into three zones, one of which is used by nudists. ⌂ FV-602
or FV-2 exit 79, signposted

At Playa de Butihondo, umbrellas and sunbeds are available for a fee.
Beach kiosks round off the offer. ⌂ FV-602, or FV-2 exit 79, after the
Hotel Fuerteventura Princess and before the Hotel Magic Life you will
find a car park on the left side of the road, from which a runway
leads down to the beach.

The snow-white main beach Playa del Matorral of Jandía is one of the
most visited beaches in the south. He was awarded the blue flag.
With a length of just under 4.5 km and an average width of 60 m, it
passes the Faro de Morro Jable lighthouse and continues to the
former fishing village of Morro Jable. In the front part, next to the
Iberostar hotel complex, begins the Saladar de Jandía, a protected
area of 115.6 hectares that extends to the SHB Maxorata hotel. The
nature reserve is one of the special ecosystems in Fuerteventura,
where salt marshes and plants have formed that grow despite the
ebb and flow of the Atlantic Ocean. For this reason, access to the
beach is only possible via landscaped paths.

On the beach, the lighthouse serves as a dividing line between the
permitted nudist beach area to the north and the non-nudist beach to
the south, towards Morro Jable. Thanks to the existing rescue and
surveillance posts, you can see if you can swim in the sea by means
of the flags. Beach kiosks, changing rooms and showers complete the
beach day. Another hotspot of beach life is the **Playa de La Solana**.

It is located between the renovated Robinson Club Jandía Playa with its new, strikingly high hotel tower and the Hotel Riu Palace Jandía Playa. You will find a beautiful beach overlooking the harbour of Morro Jable, which is also suitable for children to swim.

①Guarded beach with lifeguards, parasols and sun beds can be rented. Beach kiosk, showers and changing rooms are available. The beach offers enough space for your own beach towels and parasols, ⌂ Avenida del Saladar- 35626 Morro Jable

43 Jandía

Meanwhile Jandía is the biggest holiday resort in the south of Fuerteventura. Due to the fantastic sandy beaches, the first large hotel complexes were built in the 1960s. At that time, the transfer from the airport via the serpentine roads to the hotels took almost 5 hours. Thanks to the FV-2 motorway, which has now been upgraded, you can reach Jandía in 1.5 hours.

In the roundabout at the entrance to the village there is the impressive wind chime "Fobus" by the famous Lanzarote island artist César Manrique. Shortly afterwards you will see the skeleton of a 14 m long sperm whale on the left side.

On the long beach promenade, modern sculptures of famous island artists decorate the appearance. Restaurants, bars and shopping facilities are numerous. ⌂ Avenida del Saladar- 35626 Morro Jable,① Souvenirs and plagiarism can be bought at the African market at the end of the village.◉ Mon+ Thu 9-14, ⌂ Avenida del Saladar- 35626 Morro Jable

44 Morro Jable

At the end of the snow-white beaches of Playa de Matorral, a high volcanic rocky outcrop characterizes the village of **Morro Jable[4]**. Here is the former fishing village of Morro Jable, which you can also reach on foot along the sea or the seafront promenade. In the village you will find a variety of restaurants offering fresh fish and typical Canarian dishes.

Then follows the port of Puerto de Morro Jable, from where the ferries from Armas and Fred Olsen cross over to Gran Canaria in 3 hours and 2 hours respectively.

At the rear of the port is the Centro de Recuperación y Conservacion de Tortugas Marinas de Fuerteventura, which is dedicated to the rescue and protection of the sea turtles of Fuerteventura. It is also known as a **breeding station for sea turtles [5]** or as a "turtle kindergarten".

The plant has a surface of 800 square meters. Injured or sick turtles are treated in 12 tanks. The most common causes of their absorption are due to human activity: entanglement or ingestion of flotsam (fishing gear, raffia, plastic, etc.), ingestion or adhesion of oil and other toxic substances, accidental fishing and collisions with boats. The turtles are under medical supervision until their recovery and are then released into the sea. Another 5 basins are used for rearing young animals.

The Canary Islands are on the migration route ofsea turtles. During the summer months the loggerhead sea turtles "Caretta caretta" go to the coasts of Fuerteventura, especially to the Playas de Sotavento, to feed. Due to the increased tourism, however, they no longer find the necessary peace and quiet to lay their eggs, so the population has shrunk enormously. For the project, turtle eggs are brought from the Cape Verdean islands to Las Palmas on Gran Canaria to the ICCM marine science institute for pre-breeding and then buried on Cofete beach to hatch. After successful hatching, the babies are collected, raised in the breeding station and finally released back into the sea in Cofete.

Since turtles only reach sexual maturity after 15 years and return to the place where they were born to lay their eggs, animal welfare activists hope to settle the loggerhead turtle permanently on the island's coasts in the foreseeable future.

◍Mon-Fri 10-13, ▮free, △ Lugar Puerto de Morro Jable- 35626 Morro Jable

45 Cofete

Just before the port of Morro Jable, there is a signposted road from the FV-2 to Cofete and Punta de Jandía with the Faro de Jandía lighthouse. △ FV-2, Ctra. Punta de Jandía- 35626 Morro Jable

After 1.6 km you will find the cemetery Cementerio on the right side of the road, which is usually closed.

After that the asphalt road ends abruptly. On unpaved roads your rough and tumble adventure can begin.

The long track leads directly to the southern tip of Fuerteventura to the lighthouse Faro de Jandía, the turnoff to Cofete is marked with a big sign. If you drive towards Cofete, you will first come to the pass with the viewpoint Punto de Vista sobre Puerto de Montaña. Here you will be almost blown away by the wind, but enjoy a fantastic view of Cofete and the Barlovento coast with the beach Playa de Cofete. You follow the serpentines towards the beach. Already from a distance you will discover a small settlement with a restaurant. If you do not turn here, the slope will automatically lead you to the beach. On the right-hand side you will see the signposted building Villa Winter. First of all you will drive to the beach Playa de Cofete. Here is the small orphaned cemetery **Cementerio de Cofete[6]**. It is surrounded by a small wall covered by the sand of the beach. At the entrance there is an old locked wooden gate and on the right side a black stone block with the names of the deceased. Sand, stones and simple wooden crosses are all that decorate the graves.

Until the beginning of the 19th century, burials took place on the island under the floor of churches. If someone died far away from a church or a cemetery, the body was bound on a dromedary and transported. In the case of Cofete, 40 to 50 kilometres were covered to bring the deceased to Pájara for a Christian burial. The cemetery near the beach allowed for burials on site. The last burial took place in 1956.

The small village of Cofete was the first permanent settlement to be established in Jandía. Already in the early 19th century, the desire to colonize the region arose through the Sergeant Major of Lanzarote, José Feo de Armas and Francisco Guerra Bethencourt. They wanted to settle foreigners in the area. But this contradicted the ideas of the island council of Fuerteventura, so that in the year 1811, Cofete was originated as a settlement with local people. The settlement was carried out by tenants of the Marquis of Lanzarote, Count of Santa Coloma and Cifuentes. Its main administrators, Francisco María de León and Xuarez de La Guardia, supervised around one hundred settlers in Cofete, who were engaged in fishing and goat breeding. They lived under extremely harsh conditions and were downright exploited by the administrators, but this was not unusual at that time.

The highlight of the place is the golden, extensive sandy beach Playa de Cofete, which is in an impressive, untouched condition. It is almost 14 km long, 50 m wide and invites to long walks on the beach. Last year, Playa de Cofete was voted one of the most beautiful beaches in Europe by Tripadvisor.

➊The beach is unattended, lifeguards are not present. The sea has extremely strong undercurrents that can sweep you away within seconds. In the year 2019, a man lost his life here.

On the way back you should visit the historic **Villa Winter[7].** The entrance is at the back of the property. The exterior of the house gives an idea of the enormous splendour of that time. Large arches, elaborately worked wooden railings and numerous details inside the building, as well as a very large courtyard bear witness to the creative will of a man who had a great goal in mind.

Don Gustavo, as Gustav Winter was called by the locals, had great financial means to realize his visions here. The Spanish dictator Franco gave the German the entireJandía peninsula, which was to be used as a test site and was declared an exclusion zone. Winter was a generous promoter who brought local workers to Cofete, who worked under the strictest secrecy and had to leave the area at night. It is also likely that he took German workers with him to Fuerteventura.

The tower of the house probably served as a landmark for submarines or planes that landed on the runway of Jandía, in the area of Puerto de la Luz. A large electrical box, which was installed on the middle floor, still bears witness to this.

To this day the background for the construction of Villa Winter has not been explored. So what was the purpose of building this villa, located in the middle of this solitude, the barren land and on the coast of one of the longest beaches of the Canary Islands?

When you see the volcanic ground, you could imagine that there is a cave system under the surface. Winter had the villa built over an existing cave. It is difficult to imagine such a thing when you know that this coast is very flat in this area. But the idea of the lava caves is not as far-fetched as one might think. In Tenerife there is the volcanic cave system Cuevas del Viento, which is one of the biggest in the world and forms long tunnels with very wide spaces. Also in Fuerteventura there are some small caves of which it was already suspected that Winter wanted to use them for his further plans.

Myths or truth? - In the villa, many small details remind us of the aura of Gustav Winters. In modelled door knobs, water reservoirs and emblems, the letter W was incorporated.

In the exhibition rooms you will find the following information through a notice of the current owner: "Dear visitor, I am pleased that you have made the journey to Villa Winter. Surely you have heard many stories about this house. This building, with its inhabitants and history, was abandoned long ago to itself and decay. I am Pedro Fumero and I gave up my job, my family and my work 3 years ago when I found my uncle and my aunt here in the villa. Two old, mentally handicapped people, left to their own devices. It broke my heart and I came back to this house where I had spent much time as a child. Since that day I did not stop to maintain the house and uncover the history of the legendary house of the Winter family. I am very grateful for any support to maintain the house. Pedro Fumero."

Explore the renovated and released rooms of the old walls.

Short biography: Gustav Winter was born in 1893 in Neustadt in the Black Forest. During the First World War, he stayed abroad and visited Argentina and England, among others.

- In 1915 Gustav Winter came to Spain via England.
- In 1921 he completed his technical studies in Madrid, which he had begun in Germany, and began working on various projects.
- In 1924, at the age of 28, Engineer Winter built the Cicer power station on Las Palmas in Gran Canaria, which was opened on 21.10.1928.
- In 1933, the year Hitler came to power, Winter went to the Jandía peninsula.
- In 1937 Winter planned to build a cement factory and a fish factory in Jandía, but they were never built.
- In July 1937 Winter signed a lease for the entire Jandía peninsula with the heir of the Conde de Santa Coloma from Lanzarote. In the same year he travelled to Berlin to obtain the necessary financial support for a project, after which he returned to Fuerteventura in the summer of 1938 with a small expedition of experts on board a ship to explore the area, take photographs and produce maps.
- During this time Gustav Winter was already working as an agent for the German defence in Spain. In a meeting between Winter and the Abwehr III- Canarias it was agreed that Winter would carry out economically important projects in Jandía for the German Reich and in return receive German auxiliary personnel.
- From 1939 to 1944 he managed a shipyard of the German navy near Bordeaux in France.
- From 1939, the entire Jandía peninsula was closed and the few local people were resettled.
- At a meeting in October 1940 between Hitler and General Franco, Hitler announced that he wanted to set up a base on one of the Canary Islands, which General Franco initially rejected because of Spain's sovereign position.
- It is proven that between March and July 1941, 6 German submarine stations existed in the port of Las Palmas on Gran Canaria.
- In April 1941 the company "Dehesa de Jandia S.A." whose administrator was Gustav Winter, bought the Jandía peninsula.

- He met his wife in Madrid in 1945 and one year later the construction of Villa Winter and the extension of the road to Cofete began, which was carried out by political prisoners.
- Only in 1947 the Allies allowed the couple to return to the Canary Islands. Gustav Winter established a tomato plantation, had wells built and tried to reforest the mountains of Jandia.
- According to local people, in 1950 there were explosions on the peninsula for days on end.
- In 1962, the "Dehesa de Jandia S.A." approx. 2,300 ha of land between Morro Jable and Cofete to Gustav Winter, as compensation for the development of the peninsula. In 1966, when tourism began with the construction of the first hotels in Jandía, the Winter family was well provided for, as they received the equivalent of € 78.00 per square metre for the fallow land.
- In 1971 Winter died at the age of 78 years in Las Palmas on Gran Canaria.

☉ daily, but without obligation, since the property is privately managed, free, ♠ donations for the maintenance of the property are voluntary.

On the way back you should also visit Punta de Jandía, with the lighthouse Faro de Jandía , to explore the southern tip of Fuerteventura on your tour. To do this, go back to the Cofete turn-off and follow the course of the slope to the right.

46 Puerto de la Cruz

From Morro Jable a 20 km long dirt road leads to the southernmost tip of the island, the Punta de Jandía with the lighthouse **Faro de Jandía [8]**. Just before the lighthouse is the small settlement of Puerto de la Cruz. It was founded as a refuge for fishermen. With only 40 registered inhabitants, 2 small restaurants and a permanent caravan settlement were added to the few fishing houses. The large wind turbine has been idle since 2002. Since 2003, a diesel engine has been supplying the residents with electricity, and drinking water is transported in tankers to a central water tank.

The road leads directly to the lighthouse. It dates from the middle of the 19th century and is operated automatically. In the former house there was a permanent exhibition about the flora and fauna of the island. daily, ☉① sanitary facilities are closed.

🚍As an alternative to renting a car, you can reach the remote towns of Cofete and Punta de Jandía by public bus from the Estacíon de Guaguas bus station in Morro Jable. The bus is a Mercedes all-terrain vehicle that covers the bumpy routes relatively comfortably and in the shortest possible time. Already after 40 minutes you reach the Playa de Cofete.

If you arrive with the first transfer, you can get off at Cofete, or continue to the lighthouse. If you leave the bus, the return journey is by the next bus at 12.45 or 16.45. If you continue your journey, the bus will arrive at the lighthouse in Punta de Jandía after another 30 minutes. After a 45-minute break, the journey continues at 12.00 or 16.00 hours. When boarding, the fare of 8.70 € must be paid again. From the lighthouse we go back to Cofete. A 15-minute break is inserted here. The continuation of the journey to Morro Jable takes place at 12.45 and 16.45 hours.

① The public bus is the only alternative to the rental car to reach the southern tip of Fuerteventura. But when starting the journey it is not evident that only the one-way trip costs 8,70 € per person. In total you are on the road for 3.5 hours. Please note that there are no toilets when you get off the bus.🕑 daily, departures 10.00 and 14.00, 🚌line 111, 💰17,40 €, ⌂ Estacíon de Guaguas- Calle Cervantes, 35625 Morro Jable

47   Museum network on Fuerteventura

The Fuerteventura **Red de Museos de Fuerteventura** Museum Network includes the following institutions from north to south:

Museo de la Pesca Tradicional, in El Cotillo
Cueva del Llano, in Villaverde, currently closed
Museo del Grano La Cilla, in La Oliva
Casa Alta de Tindaya, in Tindaya
Ecomuseo La Alcogida, in Tefía
Casas de Filipito, in Altos de Guisguey
Casa Museo Unamuno, in Puerto del Rosario
La Ampuyenta, in Ampuyenta
Mirador de Morro Velosa, in Morro Velosa, under renovation
Museo Arqueológico de Betancuria, **in Betancuria**, under renovation
Museo del Queso Majorero, in Antigua
Museo de la Sal, in Las Salinas
Los Molinos, in Tiscamanita
Poblado de La Antalayita, in Pozo Negro
Faro de la Entallada, in Las Playitas

Faro Punta de Jandía, in Puerto de la Cruz

①To make sure that the museums are open during your visit, it is advisable to have someone from the hotel reception desk call you in Spanish at the central office in Mon-Fri between 08.00 and 15.00 on the number: 928 85 89 98 to confirm the opening hours. The lady at the museum headquarters speaks only broken English.

48   The history of goat's cheese

Due to a lack of historical records, it is no longer possible to determine exactly when goat's cheese production began in Fuerteventura. Fuerteventura was occupied by North African Berbers for over 1000 years, so the first settlers whose main activity was cattle breeding drew on the knowledge and experience of the Berbers. It was only through cheese production that it became possible to process, preserve and store the surplus milk.

Trade and traditional production: When Europeans were looking for trade routes to the New World across the Atlantic in the 15th century, the Canary Islands played a major role due to their favourable geographical location. The traders met on the islands to conduct regional retail and foreign trade. Unlike the other islands of the archipelago, Fuerteventura, as Isla de Señorío, had the right to levy taxes of one fifth and impose restrictions. Local, regional and inter-island trade and maritime trade took place.

Local trade was the strongest. It was conducted through shopkeepers with shops, travelling salesmen and cheese sellers.

From the years 1884-1888, detailed records were made by Dr. Rene Vernau. He described the cattle, the farm work, the shepherds and the traditional cheese production: "...The production is very simple. After milking, rennet is immediately added to the milk to make it curdle. It is filled into simple round moulds made of wood chips and palm wood, which are placed on a board. Pressure is applied to the curdled milk with the hands until the whey has escaped and the cheese has a firmer consistency. Now the cheese must be rubbed with salt and dried. When it is dried, it is so hard that you can only share it with a stone or a hammer. Often the cheese is additionally rubbed with clay on the outside, which gives it a somewhat appetizing appearance. This procedure is to prevent the cheese from hardening."

Cheese production: The tradition of handmade goat's cheese, Majorero cheese, is deeply rooted in Fuerteventura. Almost everyone who keeps goats produces cheese for their own use and sells the surplus. The following operations are necessary for production:

milking the goats, collecting the milk, adding fermenting agents and rennet, cutting the curd, draining, moulding, salting, maturing and coating the cheese.

The traditional production methods have been handed down from generation to generation. They are now being replaced by modern techniques to ensure better hygiene conditions and to be able to produce larger quantities.

The secret of goat's cheese: the Majorera goat is an indigenous breed from Fuerteventura that has adapted perfectly to the environmental conditions. From the very beginning of goat breeding, the farmers carefully selected the animals, so that in the meantime an extremely robust and resistant breed has developed. The udders of goats are very large, in animals with high milk production comparatively exaggeratedly large. The quality of the milk is very good, thick, aromatic and fatty, which is one of the most important secrets of goat cheese.

Characteristics of the cheese: The production of Canary Island goat's cheese is part of the cultural heritage of the Autonomous Community of the Islands. The cheese is made primarily from raw goat's milk, which is of high quality and gives the product its special taste, smell and appearance.

Each island produces its own cheeses, for example the cheese on Fuerteventura is called Queso Majorero, on La Palma Queso Palmero and on Gran Canaria Queso de Flor de Guía. Young goat's cheese has a light-coloured rind which turns yellowish as it matures. Spreading with paprika, olive oil or gofio gives the cheese a different appearance.

Designation of origin: The authentic Queso Majorero is labelled with a control label that guarantees the origin and quality of the raw materials, as well as the production and ageing process. The designation of origin is based on regulatory criteria which all cheeses bearing the designation must meet.

The islanders in harmony with the livestock: Before the arrival of the Europeans, the islanders called Fuerteventura Mahoh, translating my country. There is no historical record of when they arrived, but it is certain that they brought goats and shepherd dogs.

The goats were one of the most important livelihoods of the people: they were used for milk and meat production. The skins were used to make clothes and shoes, the tendons served as sewing threads and the bones as needles. Flights were constructed from leather and sticks hardened over fire. They used leather and melted tallow as a remedy and used goat milk butter to heal wounds.

Even today the shepherds of small herds still milk manually. From 60 to 100 goats, milking rooms with parallel systems are used to increase production output and hygiene conditions.

49 Cheesemakers' Queserias

Queseria Julian Diaz El Belido [1]: The cheese dairy is located in Tiscamanita. You can choose between medium mature and mature goat cheese with paprika, gofio or olive oil and cream cheese. There is also goat's yoghurt and gofio biscuits - Albajores de Gofio - with dark and light chocolate coating. You ①may need to ring the bell at the door,❹ Mon-Fri 8-16, Sat 8-14, Sun closed, ⌂ Calle San Marcos, 82- 35638 Tuineje

Queseria Benigno[2]: The cheese dairy is on the way to Ajui. In addition to the classic goat's cheese varieties, homemade Almogrote, a very piquant spread of goat's cheese, oil and paprika, is offered. ❹daily 11-16, ⌂ FV-621, km-5, 35628 Mezquez

Queseria La Pared[3]: The cheese dairy is located opposite the entrance to La Pared. In December 2019, the Regional Government of the Canary Islands once again recognised island products through the "Agrocanarias" competition, organised annually by the Canary Islands Food Quality Institute. In total, producers had registered with 173 wines, 134 cheeses, 60 gofios, 20 olive oils and 18 sea salts. The winner in the cheese category was a product from the La Pastora cheese dairy. The ripened cheese made from raw sheep's milk "La Pastorcita" with a gofio crust won first prize. ① In addition to all the cheeses, you can also try liqueur made from goat's milk,❹ Mon-Sat 9-17.30, Sun closed ⌂ FV-605, Calle Barranco de La Pared- 35628 La Pared

Queseria Maxorata[4]: The cheese dairy participates annually in the World Cheese Awards, where over 3,000 products are entered worldwide. The cheese has received the highest awards for years: In 2018-19 the Maxorata semicurado pimentón (semi-mature, paprika) was awarded the gold medal. At the 10th Edición Gourmet Quesos, which awarded prizes for the best cheeses in Spain in 2019, the cheese dairy won first prize for the Queso de oveja semicurado (semi-mature sheep's cheese) and the Tobar del Oso semicurado. At the current World Cheese Awards 2019-20, the varieties Selectum semicurado pimentón, Tobar del Oso semicurado artesano (semi-mature, handmade) and Tobar del Oso curado (matured) were awarded the silver medal. Currently, the Maxorata curado pimentón (ripened, paprika), which was awarded the 2019-20 Gold Medal, deserves special mention.☺ Mon-Fri 9-16, Sat+ Sun closed ⌂ FV-20, km 5,5, Llanos de la Higuera- 35628 Tuineje

La Casa del Queso- Queseria Cabrera Pérez [5]: The special feature of this cheese dairy is that the building complex is like a "living" museum. Here you can take a close look at all the steps of cheese production: From the raising of the goats and feeding, the modern milking plant, to the completion of the final products. In the following sales room you can taste and buy all types of cheese. ❶ Child friendly. In front of the cheese dairy a new small goat shed was built on the side, in front of which the goats and a small donkey are a nice photo motif,☺ Mon-Sat 9-18.30, Sun 10-15,🍶 free, ⌂ FV-2 > FV-50, km-7, Calle Llano- 35638 Los Alares

50   Aloe vera

Aloe Vera is a plant with healing properties that was already known to the indigenous peoples of the Canary Islands. It originates from the north and east of Africa and is widespread in the Canary Islands, where it is mainly grown in Lanzarote, Gran Canaria and Fuerteventura. The products made from the plants are considered to be of high quality.

❶ In Fuerteventura there are almost countless Aloe Vera farms. The staff in the sales outlets will inform you in detail about the mode of action and the areas of application.

51   Adventure Tours Fuerteventura

Discover all the top highlights of Fuerteventura from north to south on 5 impressive adventure tours.

51.1 The North Tour

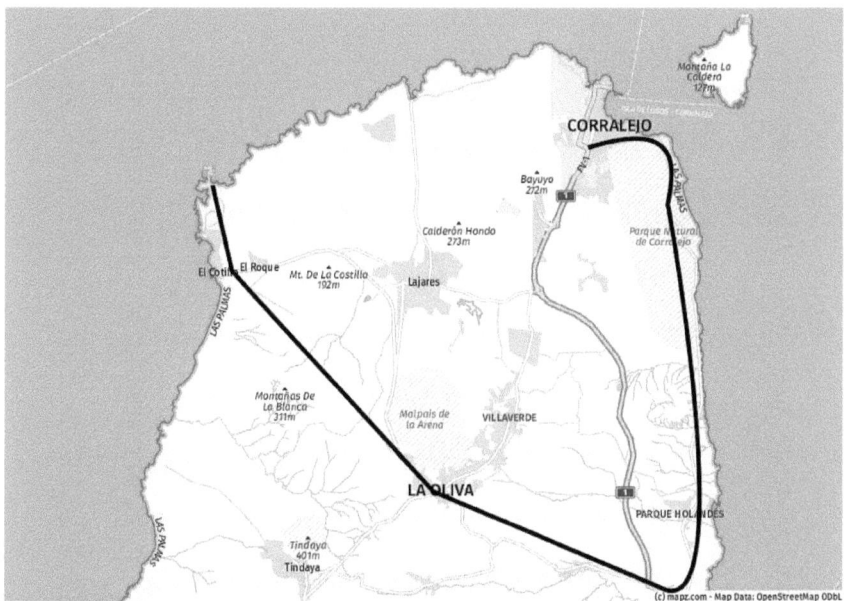

Fantastic Caribbean beaches meet shifting sand dunes and culture: This tour starts in **Corralejo** on the FV-1 > towards Playas Grandes . You drive through the Parque Natural de Corralejo, which runs directly through the shifting sand dunes. You will see the beautiful beaches Playa Bajo Negro, Playa de los Matos, Playa del Moro, Playa Alzada and Playa del Porís.

After the last beach, the white dunes change abruptly into brown volcanic mountains. Follow the road and after Casas de Jablito turn onto the FV- 102 towards La Oliva. In **La Oliva** you will visit the following sights: The church Nuestra Señora de La Candeleria, the Casa de Los Coroneles, the Ermita de Puerto Rico, the grain museum La Cilla, the art center Centro de Arte Canario- Casa Mané and the Casa del Inglés.

From here follow the FV-10 towards **El Cotillo**, visit the Castillo de El Tostón tower, see the lime kilns in the harbour and take a detour to the long Playa del Castillo.

From El Cotillo the coastal road leads north to the Fisheries Museum Museo de la Pesca Tradicional with the lighthouse Faro El Tostón. Further dreamlike bathing bays, like the Playas de Los Charcos, are located not far from the lighthouse, in northern direction.

51.2 The Discovery Tour in the centre of Fuerteventura

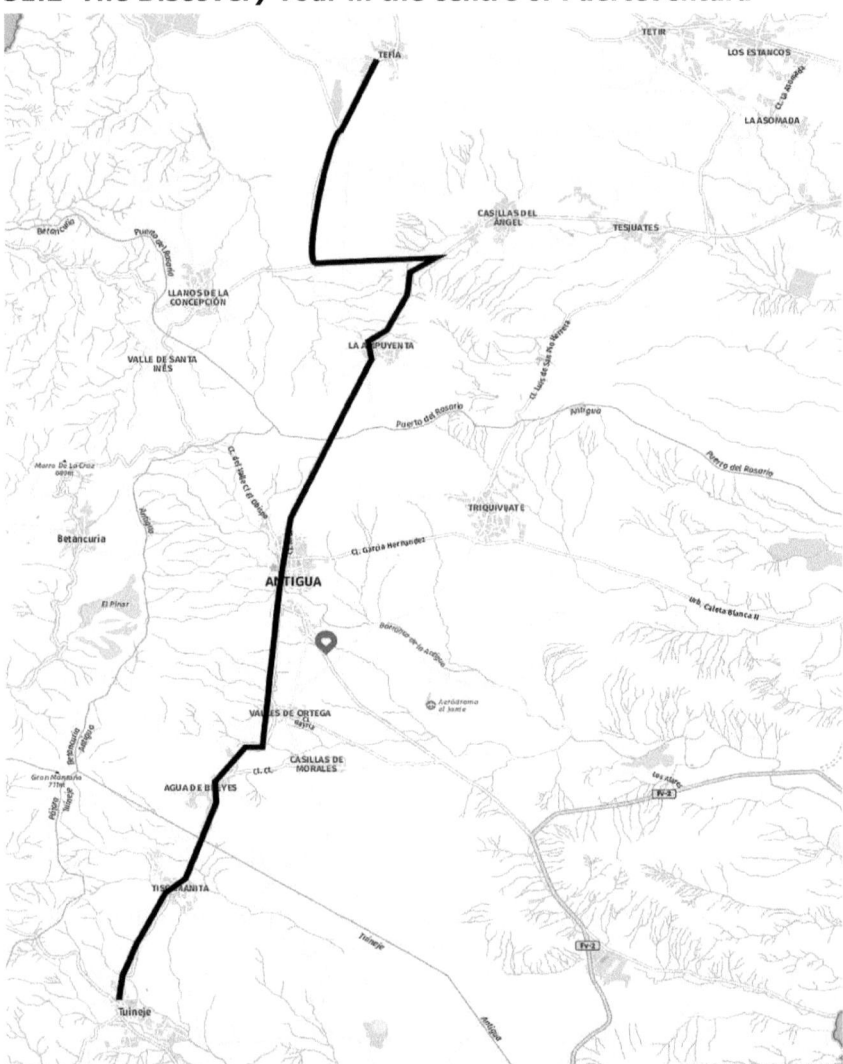

The tour starts in the village of **Tuineje**, which can be reached via the FV-20. You will visit the church of San Miguel Arcangel, with the altarpieces of the historical battle of Tamasite. From here the FV-20 leads to **Tiscamanita** with the Interpretation Centre of the Windmills - Centro de Interpretacion de Molinos. On the way you will meet the windmill Molino de Antigua with the cheese museum Museo de Queso Majorero in**Antigua**.

From Antigua the FV- 20 leads to **La Ampuyenta** with the following sights: The Hospital San Conrado y San Gaspar, the Ermita de San Pedro de Alcantara, the birthplace of Frailito Andrés and the museum house Casa Museo Doctor Mena.

To the north, take the FV- 30 and turn onto the FV- 207 to **Tefía** to the Ecomuseo La Alcogida open-air museum. The tour ends with a visit to a traditional rural village.

51.3 The perfect panoramic drive in the south

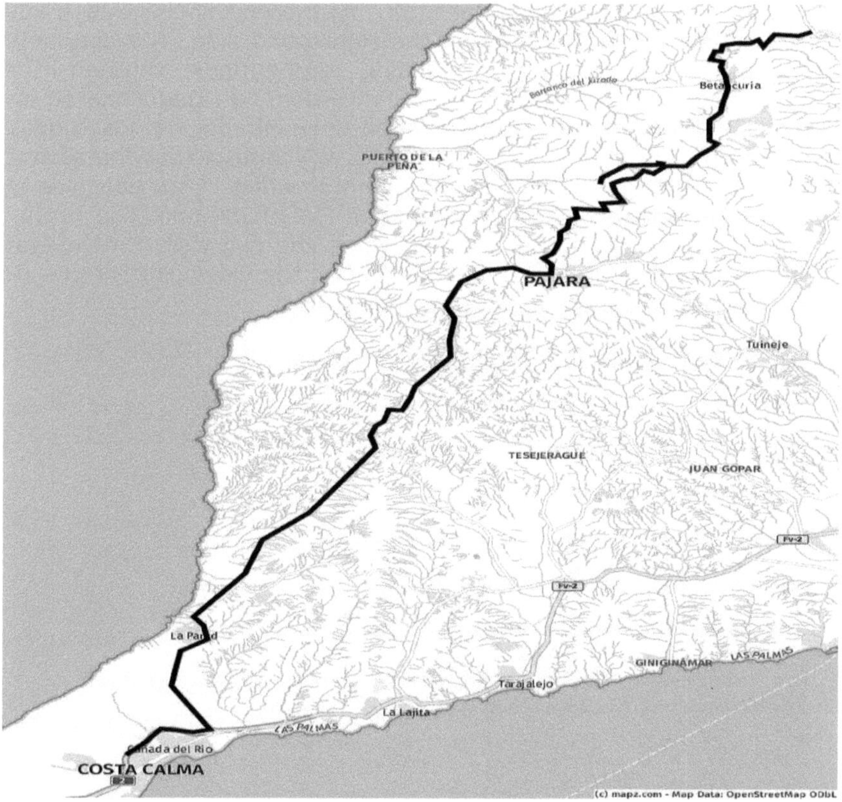

On this impressive route, you will experience the transition from a Sahara desert to softly circled and smooth volcanic landscapes and incomparable viewpoints along the road.

Coming from the south, the tour starts from **Costa Calma**, on the FV-605 towards La Pared.

Along the way, you can stop at the Mirador Astronomico de Sicasumbre for a lookout or continue your journey. Further along the road you will pass the small village of Fayagua, with covered greenhouses on the right-hand side. At harvest time, a label with the words 'Tomatoes' indicates that they are for sale.

Then, after an artificial palm tree avenue at the side of the road, the FV- 605 leads directly to **Pájara**. Here, the church Nuestra Señora de la Regla is the centre of attention.

Follow the FV-30 direction Betancuria. At the end of the village you will pass an antique lime kiln on the right-hand side. The course of the road leads you over winding serpentines through the breathtaking landscape. Shortly after the road sign Degollada de los Granadillos there is the 1st observation deck Mirador del Risco de la Peña. As you continue your journey, you will come across the second viewpoint, Mirador Las Peñitas[2], from which you can see a reservoir surrounded by palm trees. The FV-30 will take you further to the old island capital Betancuria, which you can visit. On the way to the Mirador de Morro Velosa, you will find the viewpoint Mirador de Guise y Ayose. Here the panoramic tour ends.

Space for personal notes...🖉...

51.4 The coastal tour

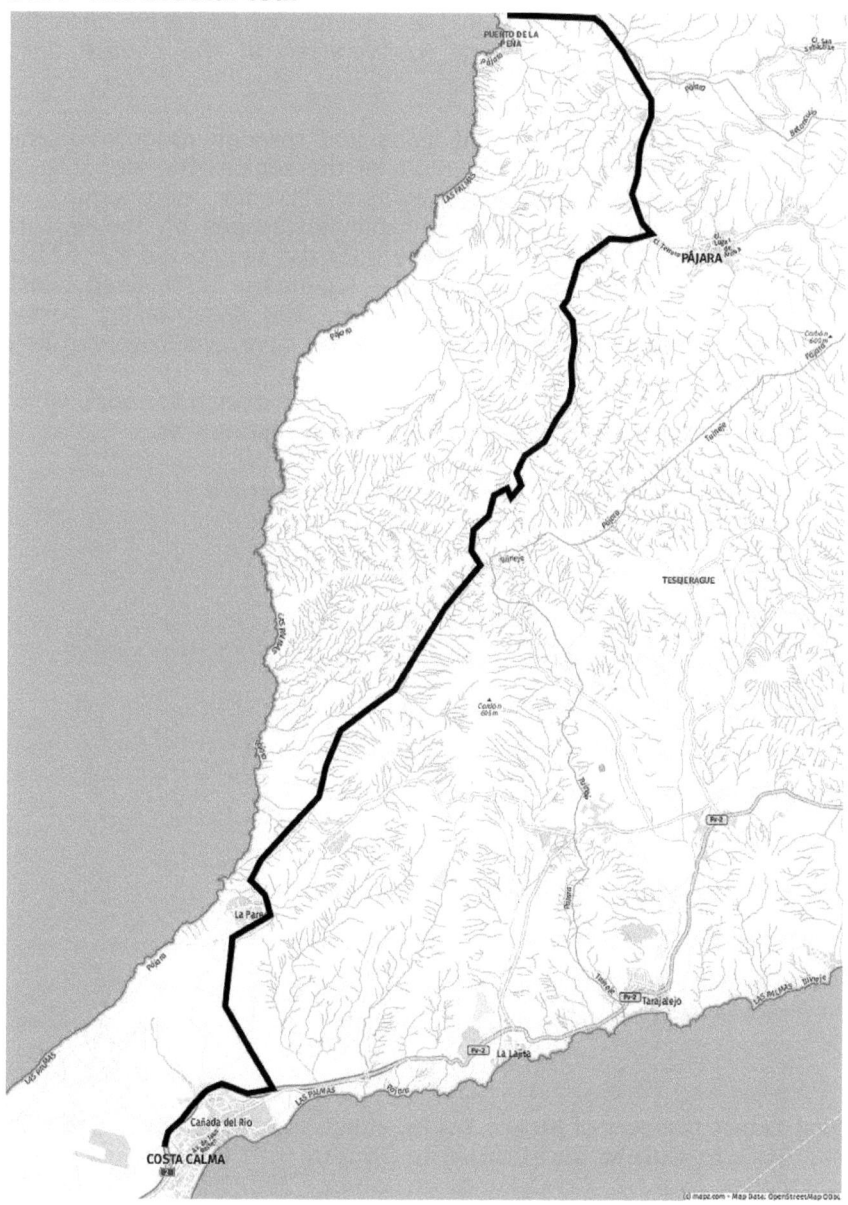

The tour starts in the south of Fuerteventura, in **Costa Calma**. From the FV- 2, take the FV-605 in the direction of La Pared. Visit the beaches in the village or try goat cheese in the cheese dairy opposite.

The further course of the road leads you through rugged volcanic landscapes, at the highest mountain of the region, the Montaña de Cardon with 691 m, to the viewpoint Mirador Astronomico de Sicasumbre. Enjoy the unique volcanic landscapes on the way to Pájara and turn off before the village onto the signposted FV- 621 to **Ajui.** Here you can sunbathe on the legendary black dead beach Playa de Los Muertos and then explore the breathtaking rocky-sandstone coast with the lime kilns and the cave, which served as a hiding place from pirates.
The tour ends with a visit to this incomparable stretch of coast, which you can conclude with a visit to the local fish restaurants.

51.5 The south tour to the tip of Fuerteventura

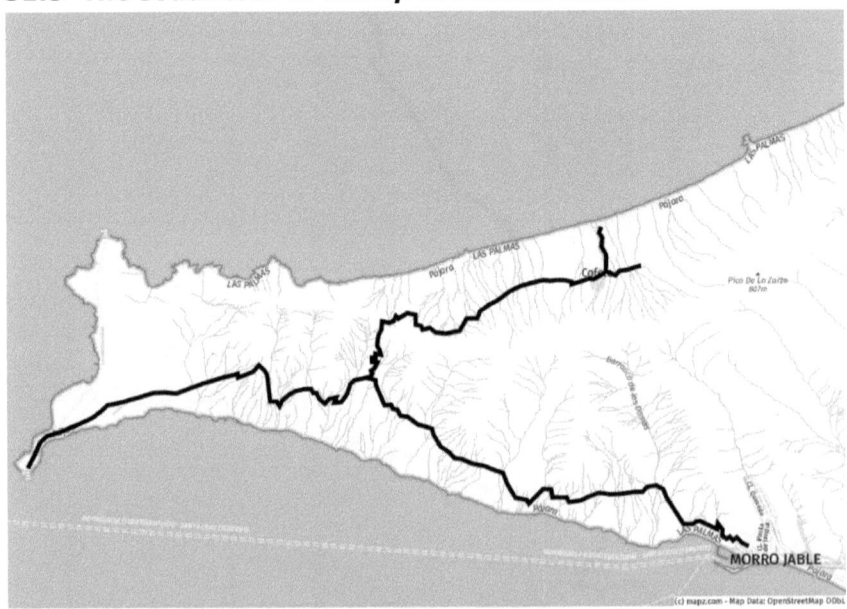

Just before the port of **Morro Jable, there is** a signposted road from the FV-2 to **Cofete** and **Punta de Jandía** with the Faro de Jandía lighthouse. ⌂ FV-2, Ctra. Punta de Jandía- 35626 Morro Jable. The long runway goes directly to the southern tip of Fuerteventura to the

70

Faro de Jandía, the turnoff to Cofete is marked with a big sign. At the pass of Cofete, with the viewpoint Punto de Vista sobre Puerto de Montaña, you have a fantastic view of Cofete and the Barlovento coast with the Playa de Cofete. Visit the historic Villa Winter and stroll along the miles of beach. Go back to the Cofete turn-off and follow the road to the right, towards El Puertito, to the lighthouse.

52 Current media

At www.kanarenmarkt.de you will find the latest information about the archipelago in a short and concise form.

All events and information about the Canary Islands can be found in the 2-week edition of the "Wochenblatt" newspaper. ①www.wochenblatt.es

The free Fuerteventura newspaper is available every 2 weeks in the exit area of the SPAR supermarkets in the south from Costa Calma.① www. fuerteventurazeitung.de

53 Short overview of markets - Mercadillos

Corralejo- Centro Comercial El Campanario ①10-14 h, Th+So
Corralejo- Baku① 8-14 h, Tue+Fri
La Oliva- Casa de los Coroneles ①10-14 h, Tue + Fri
El Cotillo- Plaza Publica ①6-21 pm, Fri
Lajares- 10-14, Sat①
Puerto del Rosario- Vega Tetir Mercadillo ①10.30-14.30, 2nd day of the month, only March, June, Sept and Dec
Caleta de Fuste ①9-14, Tue+Sa
Caleta de Fuste-El Castillo- in front of the Hotel Barceló ①10-13.30, Fri
Las Playitas- Playitas Resort ①6-22 pm, Wed
La Lajita- Oasis Wildlife Park ①9-14 hrs, Sun
Costa Calma- behind the police 9-14①, Wed + Sun
Morro Jable- Jandía- above the Robinson Club 9-14①, Mon + Thurs

54 General Information Canary Islands
Pharmacies

- There are pharmacies in all larger towns. In contrast to Germany, you can also get many medicines here without a prescription and much cheaper.

Bathing safety

- Every year people die while bathing in the Canary Islands! Please note that the Atlantic Ocean is extremely dangerous in the Canarian waters. Strong currents, undercurrents and suddenly appearing waves with strong suction effects are not uncommon. Even experienced professional swimmers have already lost their lives through carelessness. As soon as the red flag is raised, bathing is absolutely forbidden. Never go into the water just because a few people have already taken a bath. When the flag is yellow, it is already recommended to stay only in the area close to the beach. If you witness a swimming accident, do not swim after it under any circumstances. Inform the lifeguards at the guarded beaches if available, otherwise call 112.

Banks and money

- There are banks and ATMs in all larger towns. When withdrawing money with a cash card, however, there are sometimes high fees, as is the case everywhere abroad. It is best to have a small supply of cash with you and pay all other amounts with a credit card.

Bus / public transport

- The public buses on the Canary Islands are called Guaguas and run regularly between all the larger towns. You will find the departure times directly at the bus stops (Paradas). The bus tickets are quite cheap in the Canarian Islands.

Theft

- The quota of crimes is very low in the Canarian Islands, but of course there are also here "bad fingers". Therefore please do not leave anything of value open and visible. In case of theft or crime, you can call the police directly with 112. In order to be able to assert your claims with your insurance company, you must have a police protocol issued.

Shopping and business hours

- In the Canary Islands there are no fixed shop opening hours. In tourist areas, shops are often open continuously from morning to evening. These shops are also open on Sundays. In normal residential areas or big cities there is often the classic lunch break between 13-17 o'clock.

Festivals and public holidays

- In the Canary Islands many general and island-typical fiestas are celebrated. Individual communities on each island also have their local festivals and holidays. The Cannario likes to celebrate. In contrast to other countries, holidays that fall on a weekend are celebrated on the following Monday. Depending on the island and municipality, it is recommended to google on the Internet beforehand. The festivals are often very interesting, as they are celebrated with original clothes and in a highly traditional way.

Photography

- There are no specific additional rules. However, as everywhere else in the world, you should not film or record the police or military areas. Otherwise it is called with pleasure when photographing "fire freely".

church services / masses

- The Canarian population is mostly catholic and there is an Ermita or church in almost every village. The opening hours are always posted at the church, but the Sunday service at noon is always obligatory. Since many architecturally interesting churches only open during trade fairs, a visit to a trade fair is definitely recommended.

Rental car

- In the Canarian Islands, it is already possible to get some rental cars for a reasonable price. There are rental stations in every port, at the airport and also in all tourist places. Reservations can also be made in advance via the Internet.

Emergencies

- The general emergency number is 112 without area code! You can also contact the ship's reception desk directly, they have numbers of doctors, embassies, etc.

Opening hours

- In the tourist areas, the shops are usually open 7 days a week from morning to evening. But in the Canarian Islands, there is still the classic siesta, so that the shops are closed from 13-17 o'clock. As there is no law on shop opening hours as in Germany, you will always find a place to shop and linger.

Sun

- Attention. The Canary Islands are not far from the equator, so that even in December and January UV values are reached that in other countries only occur in summer. Do not be fooled by the clouds in the sky. Depending on your skin type, it is therefore advisable to use sunscreen both when going ashore and on the ship.

55 Heads up! Bathing accidents

It is frightening that every year so many holidaymakers have to lose their lives in the Atlantic. Partly out of ignorance, but also arrogance, because they think they are good swimmers. The extreme undercurrents in this part of the Atlantic Ocean are underestimated, which will be the downfall of every professional swimmer. Only within a few seconds can a "funny" wave become a deadly threat. Even in absolute proximity to the beach, the sea can suddenly retreat and develop a suction effect that even a full-grown elephant could not withstand. Guarded beaches with lifeguards, who in case of emergency put themselves in absolute danger of their lives to save the bathers, are unavoidable. Tragically, countless first-aiders have also become victims of the Atlantic last year. On average, every week a person loses his life in the Canarian waters. According to the current statistics from 2019, this also includes 3 people whose bodies have not been located in the sea.

The total number of deaths by drowning in 2019 was 57:
Gran Canaria 20
Tenerife 14
Lanzarote 10
Fuerteventura 10
El Hierro 1
La Gomera 1
La Palma 1

By activity, 63% of drowned people were bathers, followed by fishermen, divers and water sports enthusiasts. 75% of the drowned are holidaymakers, 84% of them men and 16% women. They came from Germany, England, France, Italy, Norway, Sweden, Holland, Russia, Hungary, Poland and Switzerland.